THIRD EDITION

Grammar Practice

or Elementary Students

with key

Brigit Viney
with Elaine Walker,
teve Elsworth

with CD-ROM

PEARSON
Longman

Contents

GRAMMAR

Nouns, pronouns and determiners

Nouns and determiners

Pronouns and possessives

Articles

Adjectives and adverbs

Adjectives

Adverbs

Tenses

Present tenses

Past tenses

Perfect tenses

VOCABULARY
Prepositions and phrasal verbs

Word formation

Nouns and determiners

1 book, books

one book → two book**s**   one bus → three bus**es**   one child → four **children**

- To make a singular noun into a plural noun, add *-s* or *-es*:
  book → *book**s**   game* → *game**s**   boy* → *boy**s**   bus* → *bus**es***
  match → *match**es***

  Be careful of spelling changes:
  baby → *bab**ies**   potato* → *potato**es**   knife* → *kni**ves***
- These plurals are irregular:
  man → *men   woman* → *women   child* → *children   person* → *people*
  foot → *feet   tooth* → *teeth   mouse* → *mice   fish* → *fish   sheep* → *sheep*

▶▶   **See Appendix 1: Spelling rules for plural nouns, page 169.**

P R A C T I C E

1a   **Write the plurals of the words in the box in the correct group.**

> ~~address~~   bag   birthday   box   brother   brush   bus   church
> coat   dish   dress   euro   fox   orange   pen   place   programme
> sandwich   table   tomato   toy   tree   watch   wish

-**s**:   ....

....

....

-**es**:   *addresses*   ....

....

....

1b   **Complete the table.**

Singular	Plural	Singular	Plural
beach	*beaches*	shelf	
holiday		shoe	
loaf		foot	
man		eye	
dictionary		glass	
person		potato	

2 *a banana, an orange*

a banana	**a b**ig orange	**an a**pple	**an e**xpensive pizza

- We use *a/an* before a noun when we talk about one thing or person:
  a banana (= one banana)   *an apple* (= one apple)
- We use *a* before a consonant sound: *a banana*   *a big orange*
- We use *an* before a vowel sound (*a, e, i, o, u*): *an apple*   *an expensive pizza*

PRACTICE

2a **Complete the table. Write the nouns in the box in the correct group.**

animal   answer   arm   aunt   bottle   CD   desk   e-mail   envelope
exam   exercise   film   goal   holiday   ice cream   insect   island
key   lemon   map   neighbour   octopus   omelette   office   photo
ruler   ship   town   umbrella   uncle   visitor   window

a		**an**	
		animal	

2b **Circle the correct answer.**

0 That's *a* / *an* excellent idea!

1 Is it *a* / *an* big island?

2 She's *a* / *an* American film star.

3 Are you *a* / *an* new student?

4 It's *a* / *an* ugly place.

5 Chinese isn't *a* / *an* easy language.

6 This is *a* / *an* difficult exam.

7 He's *a* / *an* important writer.

8 Have you got *a* / *an* good encyclopaedia?

9 Is that *a* / *an* nice restaurant?

10 She's *a* / *an* interesting person.

2c Complete the list of things in Luke's bedroom. Use *a* or *an*. Two things on the list are not in the picture. Can you find them?

0	...*an*... old desk	**8**	.... English dictionary
1	.... basketball	**9**	.... poster of .... football team
2	.... expensive football shirt	**10**	.... radio
3	.... bed	**11**	.... guitar
4	.... wallet	**12**	.... apple and .... banana
5	.... computer	**13**	.... small mirror
6	.... big bag	**14**	.... picture of .... elephant
7	.... alarm clock	**15**	.... long shelf

There isn't .... or .... in the picture.

3 *a DVD, the DVD*

There's **a** DVD with this magazine. I want to watch **the** DVD.
DVDs are expensive. Where are **the** DVDs?

- We use *a/an* with a singular noun when we talk about a thing but it is not clear which thing we mean:
  *There's **a** DVD with this magazine.* (It is not clear which DVD I mean.)
- We use *the* with a singular or plural noun when it is clear which thing or things we mean: *I want to watch **the** DVD.* (We know which DVD.)
- We do not use *a/an* with plural nouns:
  *He's got **a** problem.* *He's got **problems**.*

▶▶ *For more about articles, see Units 20–22.*

PRACTICE

3a **Circle the correct answer.**

A: I'm going to (0) *a /(the)* park. Do you want to come?

B: OK. Why are you going there?

A: I'm trying to take (1) *the photos /photos* of (2) *a people /people*. I'm doing (3) *an /the* art project.

B: Oh. What's it about?

A: (4) *The faces /Faces*. I want to make (5) *a /the* big picture with (6) *the photos / photos*. I need about thirty pictures. Smile!

B: Oh!

A: That's a nice photo. Look!

B: It isn't nice! Look at (7) *a /the* tree on my head! And (8) *the flowers /flowers* in my ears!

A: Don't worry. It's (9) *a /the* great picture. It's art!

B: Give me (10) *a /the* camera!

3b **Complete the conversations. Use *a*, *an*, *the* or – .**

0 **A:** Do you want to play ....*a*.... game?

 B: I don't know. What do you want to play?

1 **A:** Have you got ....*a*.... key?

 B: No. It's on the table.

2 **A:** I've got ....*a*.... idea.

 B: Oh. What?

3 **A:** Do you go to ....*a*.... rock concerts?

 B: Sometimes.

4 **A:** What's that under ....*a*.... sofa?

 B: I don't know. It's horrible!

5 **A:** Are ....*the*.... beaches here nice?

 B: Yes.

6 **A:** Is there ....*a*.... telephone near here?

 B: Yes. Near that café.

7 **A:** I'm sending Sarah ....*a*.... text message.

 B: What are you saying in it?

8 **A:** Where are Lucy and Matt?

 B: They're in ....*a*.... car. They're waiting for you.

9 **A:** Why do you like ....*the*.... horses?

 B: They're beautiful and exciting.

10 **A:** Is this CD good?

 B: Yes. ....*the*.... songs are brilliant!

4   *a glass, water*

a glass → two glasses	a car → two cars	an exam → three exams
water	rice	money

- Countable nouns can be singular or plural. We can count them and we can use numbers and *a/an* with them: *a car → two cars   an exam → three exams*
- Uncountable nouns are not usually plural. We cannot count them and we do not usually use numbers or *a/an* with them: *a̶ water   t̶w̶o̶ money*

P R A C T I C E

4a   Complete the table. Write *C* after the countable nouns and *U* after the uncountable nouns.

bread	*U*	chair		juice	
CD	*C*	umbrella		idea	
soup		rain		bus	
information		child		air	
bottle		T-shirt		book	
oil		tea		job	
friend		café		fun	
cheese		homework		programme	
food		milk		song	
cup		music		snow	
honey		flower		popcorn	
shirt		luck		box	

4b   Complete the conversation. Use *a*, *an* or – .

A: I don't eat (0) .....–..... meat.
B: Do you eat (1) .... fish?
A: Yes. And (2) .... eggs.
B: I love (3) .... fruit. I have (4) .... orange every day.
A: I have (5) .... banana at lunch.
B: Do you have (6) .... sandwich, too?
A: Yes. And (7) .... biscuit.
B: I don't like (8) .... tea. Do you?
A: Yes, but I like (9) .... sugar in it. What do you drink?
B: Oh, (10) .... coffee, usually.

5 *a/an, some, any, no*

> We've got **some** tomatoes, **some** bread and **an** orange.
> We haven't got **any** bananas or **any** cheese. We've got **no** biscuits and **no** milk.
> Have we got **any** eggs? Have we got **any** juice?

- We use *a/an* with singular countable nouns (see Unit 2):
  *We haven't got **a** melon.*   *We've got **an** orange.*
- We use *some* with plural countable nouns and uncountable nouns in affirmative sentences: *We've got **some** tomatoes.*   *We've got **some** bread.*
- We use *any* with plural countable nouns and uncountable nouns in negative sentences and questions:
  *We haven't got **any** bananas.*   *We haven't got **any** cheese.*
  *Have we got **any** eggs?*   *Have we got **any** orange juice?*
- We use *no* with singular and plural countable nouns and uncountable nouns, to mean 'not one/not any'. We use *no* with an affirmative verb:
  *We've got **no** biscuits.*   *We've got **no** milk.*
- We usually use *some* (not *any*) in questions when we offer something to someone or when we ask for something:
  *Would you like **some** biscuits?*   *Can I have **some** juice?*

PRACTICE

5a **Complete the sentences. Use *a*, *an* or *some*.**

- **0** Tom wants ....*a*......... biscuit.
- **1** There are .... bananas in the kitchen.
- **2** There's .... rice in the fridge.
- **3** I eat .... apple every day.
- **4** I'd like .... chips, please.
- **5** Laura would like .... cheese in her salad.
- **6** I've got .... sandwich for you.

5b **Complete the sentences. Use *some* or *any*.**

- **0** We need .....*some*..... onions for this soup.
- **1** Have we got .... cola?
- **2** I'm hungry. Let's make .... sandwiches.
- **3** There aren't .... tomatoes in the fridge.
- **4** We've got .... popcorn. It's in that bowl.
- **5** Is there .... water in that bottle?
- **6** We need .... flour for the cake.

5c **You and a friend are planning a party for another friend. Complete the questions. Use *a*, *some* or *any*.**

0   Have you got ......*any*....... CDs?

1   Are there .... coloured lights in the room?

2   Could I have .... money for the cake, please?

3   Are we going to have .... food?

4   Is there .... good CD player there?

5   Have you got .... balloons?

6   Can I have .... envelopes for the invitations, please?

7   Have you got .... present for her?

8   Would you like ....*some* paper for your present?

5d **Circle the correct answer.**

0   There's (no)/*any* pool in our hotel.

1   There aren't *no* /*any* people on the beach.

2   I haven't got *no* /*any* money.

3   There are *no* /*any* boat trips today.

4   Anna doesn't use *no* /*any* sun cream.

5   I've got *no* /*any* sweaters.

6   There's *no* /*any* water in this bottle.

7   I don't want *no* /*any* juice, thanks.

8   There are *no* /*any* rocks in the water.

9   There aren't *no* /*any* trees on this island.

10 There are *no* /*any* windows in our room.

5e **Natalie is going on holiday tomorrow. Complete Kate's message to her. Use *a*, *some*, *any* or *no*.**

Natalie,

For the holiday, we need (0) ......*some*...... games for the evenings. We don't need (1) .... DVDs – there's (2) ......*no*......... DVD player. For the journey, I'm going to bring (3) .... puzzle book, (4) .... coffee and (5) .... sandwiches. Have you got (6) .... magazines? There are (7) .... stops on the journey and there's (8) .... food on the train, so we can't buy magazines or sandwiches on the way.

See you tonight,
Kate

6 *a bar of chocolate, a loaf of bread*

a bar of chocolate

a loaf of bread

a piece of paper

- We cannot count uncountable nouns, but we can count:
  - the litres, grams or kilos: *a **litre** of milk   a **kilo** of meat*
  - the containers: *a **cup** of tea   three **bottles** of water*
  - the pieces: *a **piece** of chocolate   two **slices** of bread*
  - the things we buy: *a **bar** of chocolate   a **loaf** of bread*
- We can also use *a piece of* with some other nouns: *a piece of advice, a piece of furniture, a piece of luggage, a piece of music, a piece of paper*

PRACTICE

6a   Label the pictures. Use the words in the box.

bottle	bowl	can	carton	~~cup~~	glass	jar	slice	tube

0   a .... *cup* .... of coffee   **5**   a .... of cola

1   a .... of water   **6**   a .... of toast

2   a .... of popcorn   **7**   a .... of milk

3   a .... of shampoo   **8**   a .... of honey

4   a .... of toothpaste

6b   Circle the correct answer.

0   Can you get a (carton)/*piece* of orange juice from the supermarket?

1   Could I have a *bar /piece* of paper, please?

2   We need two *tins /pieces* of soup.

3   I love this *slice /piece* of music. It's beautiful.

4   How many *packets /pieces* of luggage have you got?

5   Please get two *kilos /pieces* of rice.

6   That bookcase is a beautiful *box /piece* of furniture.

7 *many, much, more*

> I haven't got **many** books.   There isn't **much** time.
> **How much** paper do you need?   There are **more** envelopes on the shelf.

- We use *many*, *much* and *more* to talk about quantity.
- We use *many* with plural countable nouns and *much* with uncountable nouns in negative sentences and questions:
  *I haven't got **many** books.   Are there **many** people in the drama club?*
  *There isn't **much** time.   Have you got **much** furniture?*
- We use *how much/how many* in questions, and *not much/not many* in short answers:
  *A: **How many** DVDs have you got?   B: **Not many**.*
  *A: **How much** paper do you need?   B: **Not much**, thanks.*
- We use *more* with plural nouns and uncountable nouns:
  *There are **more** tourists here this year.   I need **more** money.*
- We often use *some more* and *any more*:
  *I need **some more** soap but I don't need **any more** shampoo.*
- We can use *many*, *much* and *more* without a noun:
  *Are there **many**?   How **much** is it?   I need **more**.*

PRACTICE

7a **Complete the conversations. Use *many* or *much*.**

0 A: We haven't got ....*much*.... milk.
    B: I'll get some from the supermarket.

1 A: Do .... animals live in the Himalayas?
    B: I don't know!

2 A: Are there any clothes shops in this town?
    B: Yes, but not ....

3 A: I haven't got .... money.
    B: Don't worry. I can lend you some.

4 A: Have you got .... homework?
    B: Yes. And I have to revise for my exams, too.

5 A: There aren't .... tickets left.
    B: Let's buy ours now, then.

6 A: Do you watch .... television?
    B: No, not really.

7 A: Is there any information in that brochure?
    B: Well, yes, but not .... Let's visit their website.

8 A: Is he a new student?
    B: Yes, he doesn't know .... people here.

7b **Complete the questions. Use *How many* or *How much*.**

o ....*How many*..... languages are there in the world?

1 .... ice is there in the Arctic?

2 .... water is there in Lake Victoria?

3 .... states are there in the USA?

4 .... gold is there in South Africa?

5 .... canals are there in Venice?

6 .... deserts are there in China?

7 .... rain is there in Brazil every year?

8 .... volcanoes are there in the world?

7c **Circle the correct answer.**

o We've got some *much /more* exams next week.

1 *How many /How much* people are on your course?

2 Is there *many /much* information about your course on the website?

3 I don't have *many /much* free time this week.

4 I need *much /more* files for my notes.

5 There isn't any *much /more* space for these books in my bag.

6 I'm tired. I need *many /more* coffee.

7 They can't lend us any *much /more* money.

8 *How many /How much* milk do you need for the cake?

7d **Complete the conversation. Use *many*, *much* or *more*.**

A: Would you like some (o) .....*more*..... soup?

B: Yes, please.

A: And some (1) .... bread?

B: Yes, please. The soup is lovely! What's in it?

A: Meat, of course, tomatoes, potatoes, garlic and herbs.

B: How (2) .... meat do you need for it?

A: About half a kilo.

B: And how (3) .... potatoes and tomatoes?

A: Not (4) .... Just two potatoes and five or six tomatoes.

B: I can taste a bit of lemon.

A: Yes, I usually put some lemon juice in, but not (5) ....

B: Do you put (6) .... herbs in?

A: No. Just a bit of oregano and thyme.

B: Well, I love it!

A: Good! (7) .... ?

B: No, thanks! It's wonderful, but I'm afraid I can't eat any (8) ....

8 *a few, a little, a lot of/lots of*

> There are **a few** bananas in that bowl.   There's **a little** water in this bottle.
> There are **a lot of** oranges and **a lot of** bread in this bag.

- We use *a few* (= a small number of) with plural countable nouns:
  *There are **a few** bananas in that bowl.   A: Are there any eggs? B: Yes, **a few**.*
- We use *a little* (= a small amount of) with uncountable nouns:
  *There's **a little** water in this bottle.   A: Is there any cheese? B: Yes, **a little**.*
- We use *a lot of/lots of* (= a large number/amount of) with plural countable nouns
  and uncountable nouns: *There are **a lot of** oranges in this bag.*
  *There's **lots of** bread in this bag.   A: Are there any eggs? B: Yes, **a lot/lots**.*
- We can use *a lot of/lots of* like *many* and *much*, in negative sentences and
  questions: *I don't eat **a lot of** sweets.   Is there **lots of** sugar in this cake?*
  (But we also use a *lot of/lots of* in affirmative sentences.)

P R A C T I C E

8a **Complete the conversations. Use *a few* or *a little*.**

o **A:** More coffee?
   B: No, thanks. Can I have just ....*a little*........ water, please?

1 **A:** Are there any restaurants in this street?
   B: Yes, ...

2 **A:** Are your cousins here?
   B: Yes. They stay with us for .... days every summer.

3 **A:** Is there any juice in that carton?
   B: Yes, ...

4 **A:** .... people at college are really good at sport.
   B: Well, I'm not!

5 **A:** Is there any soap powder?
   B: Yes, there's .... on top of the washing machine.

6 **A:** Kirsty wants to lose .... weight.
   B: I think she looks great.

7 **A:** Have you got any ideas for your History project?
   B: Yes, ...

8 **A:** Can I have just .... sugar in my coffee, please?
   B: Of course.

9 **A:** She's only .... minutes late. Let's wait for her.
   B: She's always late!

10 **A:** Is there any bread?
    B: Yes, ... It's over there.

8b **Re-write the phrases. Use *a few, a little* or *a lot of/lots of*.**

0	3 magazines	*a few magazines*	**6**	1 g of sugar	....
1	40 sweets	....	**7**	4 CDs	....
2	5 ml of water	....	**8**	5,000 words	....
3	5 g of chocolate	....	**9**	20 l of milk	....
4	60 kg of ice	....	**10**	3 messages	....
5	5 minutes	....	**11**	150 e-mails	....

8c **Circle the correct answer.**

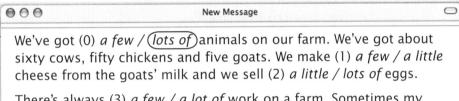

We've got (0) *a few / (lots of)* animals on our farm. We've got about sixty cows, fifty chickens and five goats. We make (1) *a few / a little* cheese from the goats' milk and we sell (2) *a little / lots of* eggs.

There's always (3) *a few / a lot of* work on a farm. Sometimes my parents only sleep for (4) *a few / a little* hours because the animals need them at night. They don't earn (5) *a little / a lot of* money, but we really like it here. It's a beautiful place. There aren't (6) *a few / a lot of* shops, but there are lovely hills and woods.

9 *all, every*

All the buses are full.	**Every** bus is full.
All children like games.	**Every** child likes games.

- We can use *all the* and *every* to talk about the things or people in a group.
- We use *all the* + plural countable noun + plural verb. But we use *every* + singular noun + singular verb. Compare:
  All the buses are full.   **Every** bus is full.
- We can use *all* and *every* to talk about things or people in general:
  All children like games.   **Every** child likes games.
- We use *all morning/afternoon/night/week/month*, etc. to mean 'the whole morning, afternoon, etc.': *We can stay at the pool **all morning**.*

 *I listen to music **all day**.*
(= I listen to music from the beginning of the day to the end.)

*I listen to music **every day**.*
(= I listen to music on Monday, Tuesday, Wednesday, etc.)

▶▶ ***For 'everything', 'everybody', etc., see Unit 18.***

P R A C T I C E

9a **Re-write the sentences. Use *all the*.**

0   Every shop is closed.   *All the shops are closed.*

1   Every cup is dirty. ....

2   Every exam starts at 9.00. ....

3   Every player in the team is important. ....

4   Every ticket here is expensive. ....

5   Every room in the hotel has a television. ....

6   Every light in the flat is on. ....

7   Every student will take the test. ....

8   Every bus stops here. ....

9b **Complete the conversation. Use *all*, *all the* or *every*.**

A: I like (0) ......*all the*...... pictures in this magazine.

B: Do you buy it (1) .... week?

A: Yes. I buy it on Saturday and I read it (2) .... afternoon. I always read (3) .... articles in it.

B: Do you keep (4) .... copy?

A: Yes. And I also enter (5) .... competition.

B: I think (6) .... competitions are silly.

9c **Circle the correct answer.**

SUNRISE STUDIOS

Come and learn how to record your own music in our studios! There are excellent recording facilities in (0) *all /*(every)*studio* and (1) *all / every* the tutors are experienced professionals from the music industry.

Here is what some people say about our courses:
'I love (2) *all / every* part of the course!'
'(3) *All / Every* session is fun and you learn a lot!'
'I like working with (4) *all / every* the different beats.'

Our courses are free for people under eighteen. The next courses start in September. There is a session (5) *all / every* Saturday for thirteen weeks. The sessions last (6) *all / every* day.

Check 1 Nouns and determiners

1 Choose and complete the sentences.

1 (a, some)
Would you like .... chips?

2 (all, every)
We visit my aunt ....
weekend.

3 (some, any)
Are there .... good tracks
on this CD?

4 (dictionarys, dictionaries)
There are two .... on that
shelf.

5 (a few, a little)
There are .... parks near
my home – three or four.

/ 5

2 Complete the conversations. Use the words in the box. You do not need all of them.

a an any many much no some the

6 A: How .... brothers and
sisters have you got?
B: I've got a brother. His name's Sam.

7 A: We're going running. Do you want to
come with us?
B: I can't. I've got .... running
shoes!

8 A: I haven't got .... money.
Only four pounds.
B: Don't worry. I can lend you some.

9 A: What's this?
B: Oh, that's .... old
photograph of my grandfather.

10 A: Where's Amy?
B: She's in .... kitchen. She's
waiting for you.

/ 5

3 Circle the correct answer.

I have breakfast at seven (11) *all / every* morning. I usually have a (12) *slice / can* of toast with honey and (13) *some / any* coffee. I never drink (14) *milk / a milk*.

For lunch and dinner, I usually have (15) *a little / a few* meat or fish, (16) *rice / a rice* or (17) *potatoes / potatos* and (18) *a little / lots of* vegetables.

In the afternoon, I sometimes have (19) *an orange / the orange* or a (20) *bar / jar* of chocolate.

/ 10

Total: / 20

✓ Self-check

Wrong answers	Look again at	Try CD-ROM
4, 17	Unit 1	Exercise 1
9	Unit 2	Exercise 2
10, 19	Unit 3	Exercise 3
14, 16	Unit 4	Exercise 4
1, 3, 7, 13	Unit 5	Exercise 5
12, 20	Unit 6	Exercise 6
6, 8	Unit 7	Exercise 7
5, 15, 18	Unit 8	Exercise 8
2, 11	Unit 9	Exercise 9

Now do **Check 1**

Pronouns and possessives

10   *I, me*

I know **him**.	**He** lives near **me**.	**She** doesn't remember **them**.

Subject pronouns	I	you	he	she	it	we	you	they
Object pronouns	me	you	him	her	it	us	you	them

⚠	Subject	Verb	Object
	I	know	**Tom.**
	I	know	**him.**

●   We always use a subject in a sentence: *He's ill.* (Not ~~Is ill.~~)
●   We use object pronouns after prepositions (*at, for*, etc.): *Wait for **me**!*

PRACTICE

10a   **Complete the conversations. Use subject pronouns.**

  0   A: Where are my CDs?   B: ......*They*...... 're in your bedroom.

  1   A: Who's that man?   B: ....'s my neighbour.

  2   A: What's this on the radio?   B: ....'s a song by Coldplay.

  3   A: How old are you?   B: ....'m eighteen.

  4   A: Where do you and Sarah live?   B: .... live near the station.

  5   A: Where's your sister?   B: ....'s in town.

  6   A: Do you like my new dress?   B: Yes! .... look beautiful!

10b   **Complete the sentences. Use object pronouns.**

  0   Anna goes to my college. I see ......*her*...... there every day.

  1   Tom and Adam are my friends. I know .... very well.

  2   We're going to the cinema. Do you want to come with .... ?

  3   Come here. I want to tell .... something.

  4   Is your brother here? I want to talk to ....

  5   My sister sometimes helps .... with my work. She's very clever.

  6   Is this your magazine? Can I look at .... ?

  7   Hurry up, boys! Your friends are waiting for ....

  8   She's beautiful! Look at ....

10c **Circle the correct answer.**

I often see my old school friends, Jessica, Ben and Emily. (0) (We)/ Us are students at the same college. Emily and (1) I / me are doing Business Studies. Jessica's studying Spanish. Ben is doing Computer Studies. (2) He / Him knows a lot about computers and I often ask (3) he / him about (4) they / them. (5) We / Us sometimes play tennis together. Emily and Ben play against Jessica and (6) I / me. (7) They / Them usually beat (8) we / us!

11 *my, your*

> Where's **my** ticket?   **Her** bag's on the chair.   **Your** hands are cold.

Subject pronouns	I	you	he	she	it	we	you	they
Possessive adjectives	my	your	his	her	its	our	your	their

- We use possessive adjectives before nouns, to talk about something that belongs to someone: *Where's **my** ticket?   **Her** bag's on the chair.*
- We often use possessive adjectives with parts of the body: ***Your** hands are cold.*

P R A C T I C E

11a **Emma is showing her photos to a friend. Match the sentences.**

o	This is me.	[f]	**a**	His name's Simon.
1	This is my sister.	☐	**b**	You can see our heads behind Rob and Tim.
2	This is me and Rachel.	☐	**c**	Your eyes are shut, I'm afraid.
3	These are my cousins.	☐	**d**	Her name's Rachel.
4	This is my brother.	☐	**e**	Their names are Ben and Holly.
5	And that's you!	☐	**f**	You can only see my feet above the water.

11b **Complete the conversation. Use possessive adjectives.**

A: Could I borrow (0) ...*your*.... CD player, please?

B: I'm sorry. (1) .... headphones are broken. You can borrow (2) ....
MP3 player if you like.

A: No, thanks. I want to listen to this CD. Richard and I are learning a song from it
for (3) .... gig next month.

B: Oh, right. How's (4) .... band?

A: It's great, thanks. I like playing with Richard.

B: Matt, Dylan and Kimberley have a band now, too.

A: Really? Are they good?

B: (5) .... songs are all right. Kimberley sings, and she's great! (6) ....
voice is fabulous! Matt doesn't play brilliantly – or (7) .... guitar isn't very
good.

A: (8) .... guitar isn't very good either, but I can't buy a new one.

12 *Sarah's bag*

That's Sarah**'s** bag.   The students**'** coffee bar is on the first floor.
The children**'s** names are Rose and Tom.   Emma and Kate**'s** father is a teacher.

- We use the possessive *'s* to talk about what belongs to people, and sometimes
  animals, but not things (for things, see Unit 13): *That's Sarah's bag.*
- We add *'s* to all singular nouns, and to plural nouns that do not end in -*s*:
  My aunt's house is near here.   The children's names are Ray and Tom.
- We add an apostrophe (*'*) to plural nouns that end in -*s*:
  The students' coffee bar is on the first floor.

 Emma and Kate's father is a teacher.
(Not *Emma's and Kate's father is a teacher.*)

P R A C T I C E

12a **Complete the phrases. Use *'s* or *'*.**

0 my brother.*'s*.... bike

1 the boys...... names

2 Sarah and John...... aunt

3 the cat...... basket

4 those ladies...... bags

5 Ben...... birthday

6 my friends...... house

7 Lisa...... phone number

8 Mr Smith...... shop

9 my parents...... bedroom

10 Jo...... book

11 my cousins...... dog

12 Ian...... car

13 men...... clothes

12b **Re-write the sentences. Use the words in brackets.**

0 Those are her glasses. (my sister)   *Those are my sister's glasses.*

1 Where's his wallet? (Andrew)   ....

2 What are their names? (those men)   ....

3 Are these their photos? (your friends)   ....

4 Her name's Jet. (the dog)   ....

5 Where are their CDs? (Amy and Kim)   ....

6 That's their cat. (our neighbours)   ....

12c **Circle the correct answer.**

A: Where's (o) *Anna's* / *Annas'* house?

B: It's near (1) *Jamie's and Craig's* / *Jamie and Craig's* school.

A: Is that near your (2) *dad's* / *dads'* office?

B: Yes. It's behind the (3) *children's* / *childrens'* playground.

A: Is this your (4) *mum's* / *mums'* CD?

B: Yes. It's nice, isn't it?

A: Yes. My (5) *parent's* / *parents'* CDs are awful! They like really horrible music!

B: Well, your (6) *brother's* / *brothers'* CDs are very good.

A: Yes, but he never lets me borrow them!

12d **Look at Becky's family tree and complete the sentences. Use the words in the box.**

| brother | cousins | father | Michael and Liz | ~~mother~~ | mother | parents |

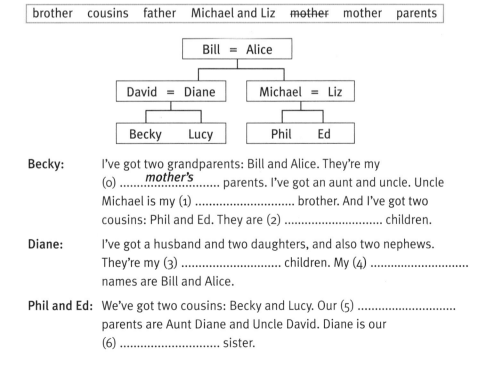

Becky: I've got two grandparents: Bill and Alice. They're my (o) ... *mother's* ... parents. I've got an aunt and uncle. Uncle Michael is my (1) .... brother. And I've got two cousins: Phil and Ed. They are (2) .... children.

Diane: I've got a husband and two daughters, and also two nephews. They're my (3) .... children. My (4) .... names are Bill and Alice.

Phil and Ed: We've got two cousins: Becky and Lucy. Our (5) .... parents are Aunt Diane and Uncle David. Diane is our (6) .... sister.

13 *the end of the road, the car keys*

> The park is at the **end of the road.**   Where are the **car keys**?

- We use *of* to say that one thing is part of another. We often use it with the words *side, top, bottom, back, front, end* and *beginning*:
  The park is at the **end of** the road.   Their house is at the **top of** the hill.
- We do not always use *of* to say that something is part of something else. We can use noun + noun: *Where are the **car keys**?* (Not ~~the keys of the car~~)

P R A C T I C E

13a **Complete the sentences. Use the words in the box and *of the* if necessary.**

> ~~book~~   centre   class   corridor   film   screen   window

0   The answers are at the back ......*of the book*...... , on page 121.

1   I can't see very well because the light's shining on the computer ....

2   The toilets are at the end .... , on the left.

3   I don't like sitting at the front ....

4   There's a nice black coat in that shop ....

5   Hurry up! I don't want to miss the beginning .... !

6   Is this the way to the town .... ?

13b **Complete the letter. Use the words in brackets and *of the* if necessary.**

Hi, Laura!

We're staying in an old house in the country and we're having a few problems! The (0) ......*bathroom light*...... (bathroom / light) doesn't work and we can't shut the (1) .... (kitchen / door). All the furniture's very old and the (2) .... (living room / curtains) are a horrible colour. And there's an awful picture of a cat at the (3) .... (top / stairs).

At the (4) .... (back / house) there's a small garden. It's pretty and I can see it from my (5) .... (bedroom / window). At the (6) .... (side / house) is a little path to the river. The river's lovely and we walk along it every day. We don't want to stay in the house! See you soon.

Love,

Emily

14 *mine, yours*

| This isn't Lucy's bag. It's **mine**.   I've got my mobile. Have you got **yours**? |

Possessive adjectives	my	your	his	her	its	our	your	their
Possessive pronouns	mine	yours	his	hers	–	ours	yours	theirs

We use possessive adjectives (*my, your,* etc.) with nouns. We use possessive pronouns (*mine, yours,* etc.) instead of *my/your* + noun. Compare:
*We've got **our exams** today and they've got **theirs** tomorrow.*
*That's **my bag**. Where's **yours**?*

PRACTICE

14a Complete the sentences. Use possessive pronouns.

  0 Don't eat those sweets! They're ......*mine*...... ! (my sweets)

  1 Those aren't his glasses. They're .... (her glasses)

  2 Their team colours are red and white and .... blue and white. (our colours)

  3 Which room is .... ? (your room)

  4 My bag is here and .... is under that seat. (his bag)

  5 Please give this DVD to Scott and Robert. It's .... (their DVD)

  6 Why are you worried about your exams? I'm not worried about .... (my exams)

  7 My suitcase is black and .... is blue. (her suitcase)

  8 This is my dictionary. Where's .... ? (your dictionary)

14b Circle the correct answer.

  A: I like (0) *their*/*theirs* songs. Do you?
  B: Yes, but I prefer (1) *our* /*ours*.

  A: (2) *Her* /*Hers* car is brilliant!
  B: (3) *Your* /*Yours* is nice, too!

  A: Katherine lives in New Street.
  B: Really? Tom and Anna live there, too. What number's (4) *her* /*hers* house?
  A: Thirty two. What number is (5) *their* /*theirs*?
  B: Twenty one. It's the same as (6) *our* /*ours*, but we live in Davy Road, of course!

  A: Who's (7) *your* /*yours* football coach?
  B: Mr Harrison. Who's (8) *your* /*yours*?

15 *this, that, these, those*

This bag's nice.	Do you like **these** glasses?
That's the bathroom.	Do you know **those** boys?

- We use *this* and *these* to talk about things or people that are near to us. We use *this* + singular/uncountable noun, and *these* + plural noun:
  This bag's nice.   Do you like **these** glasses?

- We use *that* and *those* to talk about things or people that are not near to us. We are looking at them, or pointing to them. We use *that* + singular/uncountable noun, and *those* + plural noun:
  That's the bathroom.   Do you know **those** boys?

- We can use *this, that, these* and *those* as pronouns (without a noun) when we talk about things (not people): *Do you like **this**?   Are **those** yours?*

- We can also use *this* and *that* as pronouns when we introduce someone, or when we ask about someone: **This** *is my friend, Kate.   Who's **that**?*

- We use *this* and *these* for things that we are experiencing now. We use *that* and *those* for things that we experienced in the past:
  This *programme's great.* (I'm watching the programme now.)
  I didn't like **that** *programme.* (The programme has finished.)

PRACTICE

15a Circle the correct answer.

  0 A: Does Kelly's cousin work in (*this*)/*these* shop?
  B: Yes, she does. There she is.

  1 A: Are *this* /*these* letters for me?
  B: No, they're for Rosie.

  2 A: Is *that* /*those* a good book?
  B: Yes, it's very interesting.

  3 A: *That* /*Those* CDs are very cheap.
  B: Yes, but we can only buy one. We've got £10.

  4 A: I want to buy *this* /*these* computer game.
  B: How much is it?

  5 A: Are *that* /*those* your keys?
  B: No, I think they're Sarah's.

  6 A: Are *this* /*these* pens good for drawing?
  B: Yes, but they're very expensive.

  7 A: *This* /*These* is my brother, Sam.
  B: Hi, Sam.

  8 A: I like *that* /*those* blue T-shirt.
  B: Hmm ... the red one's nicer.

15b **Look at the pictures and complete the sentences. Use *this, that, these* or *those*.**

This .... is a good magazine. Would you like to read it?

Yes, please. Would you like to read *these* .... ?

Can I leave .... glass here?

Could you put it on .... shelf, please?

Do you like .... candles?

They're OK, but I prefer ....

Who's .... ?

...............'s George, David's brother.

15c **Complete the sentences. Use the words in the box.**

> this cake   that cake   ~~this exam~~   ~~that exam~~   this match   that match
> these trips   those trips   these tennis lessons   those tennis lessons

o Did Mark pass ....*that exam*............ last week?

oo Don't worry. ....*This exam*............'s very easy.

1 We can win .... The other team isn't playing well.

2 We didn't play well in .... and we lost 4–0.

3 .... was lovely. I had two pieces!

4 .... is delicious. Would you like some?

5 I love .... The coach is really good.

6 I didn't learn anything in .... last term. We didn't play much.

7 We enjoyed .... to London last year. They were exciting.

8 I like .... to the coast. They're very relaxing.

16 *It's Tom's.*

A: Whose is this?	B: It's **Tom's**.
A: Is this your laptop?	B: No, it's my **parents'**.

We use *'s* and *'* to talk about possession (see Unit 12). We can use them without a noun when it is clear what we mean:
A: Is this your laptop? *B: No, it's my parents'.*

⚠ We use *whose* to ask about possession: ***Whose** is this?*

▶▶ **For 'whose', see Unit 74.**

PRACTICE

16a Look at the pictures and complete the sentences.

0 The ball is .... *Paul's* ....

1 The small bag is ....

2 The envelope is ....

3 The big box is ....

4 The racket is ....

5 The small box is ....

6 The big bag is ....

16b Look at the table and complete the conversations.

	MP 3 player	CDs	dog	car	bag	DVDs
my sister	✓					
my parents		✓				
my brother				✓		
my cousins			✓			
my aunt					✓	
my friend						✓

0 **A:** Is this your MP3 player? **B:** No, it's .... *my sister's* ....

1 **A:** Are these your CDs? **B:** No, they're ....

2 **A:** Is that your dog? **B:** No, it's ....

3 **A:** Is that your car? **B:** No, it's ....

4 **A:** Is that your bag? **B:** No, it's ....

5 **A:** Are these your DVDs? **B:** No, they're ....

17 *one, ones*

> That bag's Sarah's and this **one**'s mine.
> I don't like the yellow flowers, but I like the blue **ones**.
> Tom's flat is the **one** with the green door.

- We can use *one* instead of repeating a singular (countable) noun and *ones* instead of repeating a plural noun: *That bag's Sarah's and this **one**'s mine.*
  *I don't like the yellow flowers, but I like the blue **ones**.*
- We often use preposition + noun after *one/ones*:
  *Tom's flat is the **one with the green door**.*

PRACTICE

17a Complete the conversations. Use the words in brackets and *one* or *ones*.

0 A: Is this your bag?   **B:** No, mine's the .... *red one* .... (red)

1 A: Are these shirts clean?   **B:** No, but .... are. (those)

2 A: Those maps are Stuart's.   **B:** Are .... his, too? (these)

3 A: Is that our bus? The 111?   **B:** No, ours is .... (this)

4 A: Are the pens in that drawer?   **B:** No, they're in .... (that)

5 A: I like the blue earrings.   **B:** The .... are nicer. (pink)

17b Read the text and complete the conversation. Use *one* or *ones*.

> Anna's building is the building next to the two restaurants. The restaurants are near the Italian café. Anna's balcony is the balcony with a blue table and chairs. The balconies with the plants belong to some older people. Anna's flat is the flat with the blue door. Anna's grandparents live in the building opposite the bookshop.

Rosie: Is your building the big one opposite the supermarket?

Anna: No, it's (0) .... *the one next to the two restaurants* .... Do you know them?
They're (1) ....

Rosie: Yes, I know them. So, your building is the one with the nice balconies!
Some of those have beautiful plants! Is your balcony one of those?

Anna: No, ours is (2) ....
(3) .... belong to some older people.
Our flat's on the top floor. It's (4) ....

Rosie: Do your grandparents live in your building?

Anna: No, they live in (5) ....

Rosie: Oh, yes – I know the one you mean.

18 *something, everything*

For things	There's **something** in my shoe.	He doesn't know **everything**!
For people	There's **somebody** at the door.	Is **everybody** here?
For places	He lives **somewhere** in London.	She follows him **everywhere**.

● We use *something, somebody/someone* and *somewhere* in affirmative sentences:
  *There's **something** in my shoe.*   *He lives **somewhere** in London.*

● We use *everything, everybody/everyone* and *everywhere* in affirmative and negative sentences, and questions:
  *She follows him **everywhere**.*   *He doesn' t know **everything**!*   *Is **everybody** here?*

⚠ *somebody = someone* and *everybody = everyone*
  *There's **somebody/someone** at the door.*   *Is **everybody/everyone** here?*

PRACTICE

18a Circle the correct answer.

  0 I like *something /(everything)* in this shop, but I can only buy one thing.

  1 There are flowers *somewhere /everywhere* in the hotel, so all the rooms are very pretty.

  2 There's *something /somewhere* about your friend Leanne in the paper.

  3 There's *somebody /everybody* in the living room. He wants to see you.

  4 Our hotel is *somewhere /everywhere* in the city centre.

  5 Can you help with the cooking? I can't do *something /everything*!

  6 Is *everybody /everything* in your family tall?

  7 Listen. *Somebody /Something*'s singing. I think it's Jill.

  8 I want to go *everything /everywhere* in the world.

18b Complete what Anna says. Use *something, somebody, somewhere, everything, everybody* or *everywhere*.

I want to be a doctor. I like working with people and I think that
(0) ....*everything*...... about the human body is fascinating. I'd like to work
(1) .... in Africa. There's an organisation that works with
children there. I know (2) .... who works for it. I'd like to work
for it, too.

There are a lot of health problems (3) .... in the world and I
want to do (4) .... about them. I can't help
(5) .... , of course, but I want to help some people.

19 *anything, nothing*

For things	There isn't **anything** in this box.	There's **nothing** in that bag.
For people	Is **anybody** at home?	There's **nobody** in the kitchen.
For places	We aren't going **anywhere**.	The cat's **nowhere** in the house!

- We use *anything, anybody/anyone* and *anywhere* in negative sentences and questions: *There isn' t* **anything** *in this box.*   *Is* **anybody** *at home?*
- We use *nothing, nobody/no one* and *nowhere* with affirmative verbs. We use them to mean 'not anything, not anybody,' etc.:
  There's **nobody** *in the kitchen. (= There isn' t anybody in the kitchen.)*

 anybody = anyone and *nobody = no one*
Is **anybody/anyone** *at home?*   *There' s* **nobody/no one** *in the kitchen.*

P R A C T I C E

19a Circle the correct answer.

  0 I can't eat (anything)/ *nothing*.

  1 Kate doesn't know *anybody /nobody* here.

  2 Our names are *anywhere /nowhere* on this list.

  3 There's *anything /nothing* about our town on this website.

  4 He doesn't walk *anywhere /nowhere*. He always drives.

  5 There's *anyone /no one* at the reception desk.

  6 She never tells me *anything /nothing*.

  7 We can't go *anywhere /nowhere*. We must stay here.

  8 There's *anything /nothing* in this box. It's empty.

19b Complete the conversation. Use the words in the box.

| anybody | ~~anything~~ | anything | anywhere | nobody | nothing | nowhere |

A: Hi, Anna. I'm in town. It's very quiet here. What are you doing?

B: I'm not doing (0) ......*anything*...... . It's very quiet here, too. There's
(1) .... at home with me. Are you with (2) .... ?

A: No, I'm not. I'm alone and I'm standing outside a clothes shop. The clothes are
horrible! I don't like (3) .... in the window. Listen, Anna, I can't
find my new sunglasses (4) .... Are they at your house? On the
table?

B: No, there's (5) .... on the table. Sorry.

A: Oh dear! They're (6) .... at home!

B: Don't worry. You'll find them. Maybe Isabel's got them.

Check 2 Pronouns and possessives

1 Circle the correct answer.

1 Are these *your / yours* sunglasses?

2 He lives *everywhere / somewhere* in Scotland.

3 That's my *brother's / brother* bike.

4 *This / These* trainers are very expensive.

5 His *sister's / sisters'* names are Beth and Hannah.

/ 5

2 Complete the conversation. Use the words in the box.

everybody   he   him   his   nobody

A: Where's Daniel? Is (6) .... here? I want to talk to (7) ....

B: I don't know. I think he's outside.

A: No, there's (8) .... outside. (9) ....'s in here, in the cafeteria.

B: Oh – there's Joe, (10) .... friend. Let's ask him. Joe!

/ 5

3 Choose and complete the sentences.

11 (my father's, my fathers')
This isn't my car. It's ....

12 (back, back of)
There are some envelopes at the .... that drawer.

13 (one, ones)
I've got some black shoes, but I haven't got any brown ....

14 (their, theirs)
Our car's old but .... is new.

15 (anything, nothing)
I can't buy .... ! I've got no money!

/ 5

4 Complete the conversations. Use one word in each gap.

16 A: Is that Jack's cousin?
   B: Yes. .... name's Lisa, I think.

17 A: Hi, Lucy. Have you got any pictures in this exhibition?
   B: Yes – one. It's the little .... over there.

18 A: Do you like my new earrings?
   B: Yes! ....'re beautiful!

19 A: Look. Lee's notebook's under that chair.
   B: That's not Lee's notebook. It's .... It's got my name on it!

20 A: Is that her house?
   B: No. Hers is at the end .... the road.

/ 5

Total: / 20

Self-check

Wrong answers	Look again at	Try CD-ROM
6, 7, 18	Unit 10	Exercise 10
1, 10, 16	Unit 11	Exercise 11
3, 5	Unit 12	Exercise 12
12, 20	Unit 13	Exercise 13
14, 19	Unit 14	Exercise 14
4	Unit 15	Exercise 15
11	Unit 16	Exercise 16
13, 17	Unit 17	Exercise 17
2, 9	Unit 18	Exercise 18
8, 15	Unit 19	Exercise 19

Now do **Check 2**

Articles

20 *a shirt, the shirt*

> There's **a** shirt here and **a** sweater. **The** shirt's mine and **the** sweater's Rob's.

We use *a/an* with a singular noun when we talk about something for the first time. We use *the* with a singular or plural noun when we talk about something for the second time:
*There's **a** shirt here and **a** sweater. **The** shirt's mine and **the** sweater's Rob's.*
*Here are my shirts and sweaters. **The** shirts are clean but **the** sweaters are dirty.*

PRACTICE

20a Circle the correct answer.

A: This website has some good information and (0)@/*the* nice message board.
B: Really? What do people write about on (1) *a /the* message board?
_____
A: Oh, look – here's (2) *an /the* e-mail from Lisa. And this one's from Ryan.
B: What's (3) *an /the* e-mail from Lisa about?
_____
A: That's my brother's laptop. He's got (4) *a /the* desktop at work.
B: Does he use (5) *a /the* laptop for work?
_____
A: I want to buy (6) *a /the* book and (7) *a /the* CD on that website.
B: What's (8) *a /the* book about?
A: It's about (9) *a /the* man who lives on (10) *an /the* island in the Pacific.
_____
A: There's (11) *a /the* laptop here and (12) *a /the* bag. Are they yours?
B: No, they're Becky's.

20b Complete the extract from a guidebook. Use *a* or *the*.

Chester is (0) .....*a*........ beautiful town in the north of England. There are high walls of red stone around (1) .... city. You can walk on top of (2) .... walls! Chester has (3) .... cathedral, (4) .... castle, (5) .... Roman theatre, some Roman gardens, (6) .... famous clock, (7) .... park and (8) .... river. (9) .... Roman gardens are beautiful. (10) .... clock is in the centre of the town. It is more than 100 years old. (11) .... park has some lovely trees and plants. (12) .... river is very pretty, with a lot of trees near it.

21 *a shop, the post office*

> She works in **a** shop in London.   I live near **the** post office.

- We use *a/an* when we talk about a thing but we do not say which thing we mean (see Unit 2):
  *She works in **a** shop in London.* (We are talking about one shop, but we do not say which one.)
  *We're going to stay in **a** hotel.* (We are talking about one hotel, but we do not say which one.)

- We use *the* when it is clear which thing we mean because there is only one:
  *I live near **the** post office.* (There is only one post office in this area.)
  ***The** moon is beautiful!* (There is only one moon.)

P R A C T I C E

21a **Complete the sentences. Use *a*, *an* or *the*.**

0 We're going to meet Jonathan at ....*the*.......... airport. Do you want to come?

1 I like swimming in .... sea.

2 We've got some eggs. Let's make .... omelette.

3 Has your school got .... swimming pool?

4 .... air isn't clean here.

5 I want to travel round .... world.

6 Are you going to have .... party for your birthday?

7 Who's .... president of France?

8 I've got .... appointment at ten.

9 Mark's in .... bathroom.

10 There's .... bus stop near my house, so I can get to town very easily.

21b **Circle the correct answer.**

$\mathscr{Sweden}$ is (0) *a* / *the* country in the north of Europe. It is in (1) *a* / *the* European Union. (2) *A* / *The* official language is Swedish, but many people speak English. In the north of Sweden, (3) *a* / *the* sun does not set for some days in the summer, so (4) *a* / *the* sky is light all the time!

Stockholm is (5) *a* / *the* capital of Sweden. It is (6) *a* / *the* beautiful city. It has lots of beautiful historic buildings, museums, restaurants and cafés. Tourists can buy (7) *a* / *the* card for free entry to all Stockholm's museums and free travel on (8) *a* / *the* bus and metro system.

22 *a good book, the piano, tennis*

> That's **a** good book.   Rob plays **the** piano.   We sometimes play tennis.

- We use *a/an* when we:
  - talk about a person's job: *Jenny's **a** teacher.*
  - describe something or someone with the verb *be*: *That's **a** good book.*
- We use *the* with:
  - musical instruments: *Rob plays **the** piano.*
  - the names of cinemas, theatres, museums and hotels:
    the *Picturehouse*   **the** *Globe Theatre*   **the** *British Museum*   **the** *Hilton*
  - plural names of people: ***the** Johnsons* (= the Johnson family)
- We do not use *a/an* or *the* with:
  - sports and games: *We sometimes play tennis.   Do you play chess?*
  - school subjects: *I like Biology but I don't like Maths.*
  - meals: *When's dinner?   Sarah's coming to lunch.*
  - the names of streets: *North Road   Baker Street*
  - the names of countries, cities and towns: *Japan   Rome   Cambridge*

 We use *the* with the names of these countries:
the *United States of America* (**the** USA)   **the** *United Kingdom* (**the** UK)

PRACTICE

22a Circle the correct answer.

   0 **A:** What's that noise?
      B: Nick's learning to play *a /(the)* violin.

   1 **A:** Does your sister work?
      B: No, she's *a /the* student.

   2 **A:** We're going to see a play at *a /the* National Theare on Saturday. Would you like to come with us?
      B: Oh, yes – thank you.

   3 **A:** Let's go to the cinema tonight.
      B: Yes, that's *a /the* good idea. Let's meet at the station at seven.

   4 **A:** Which hotel are you staying at?
      B: *A /The* Palace.

   5 **A:** Can you play *a /the* guitar?
      B: No, I can't.

   6 **A:** Do you know the way to *a /the* Natural History Museum?
      B: No, I don't. Let's ask that girl over there.

22b Complete the sentences. Use *a* or *the*.

0   ....*The*.... Potters live in Foxton. Mr Potter has a shop there.

1   This is .... very busy street.

2   Jack plays .... drums in a band.

3   James is taking the children to .... Transport Museum tomorrow.

4   Ben's .... journalist. He works for a national newspaper.

5   Are .... Atkinsons coming to your party?

6   When are Keith and Carol coming back from .... USA?

7   I'm going to see a film at .... Odeon on Saturday.

8   Is your room at .... Sheraton nice?

22c Complete the sentences. Use *the*. If a sentence does not need *the*, put a tick (✓) in the box.

0   I'm sure we'll have a great time in .... London next week!   ☑

1   Tim and I are going to go to .... Science Museum.   ☐

2   Emily isn't going to come to the museum. She isn't interested in ....   ☐
science!

3   On Saturday, we're going to see a play by Shakespeare at ....   ☐
Globe Theatre.

4   Then we're going to have .... dinner at a famous Chinese restaurant.   ☐

5   I'm going to go shopping in .... Oxford Street, of course!   ☐

6   We're going to stay at .... Garden Court. It's a very nice hotel in west   ☐
London.

22d Complete the conversation. Use *a*, *an*, *the* or – .

A: What are you doing tomorrow? Are you going anywhere?

B: Yes. We're going to visit some friends in (0)....–..... York. They're (1) ....
Campbells – my Scottish friends.

A: That's nice. York's (2) .... beautiful city. What are you going to do there?

B: Oh, not much. Spend time with my friends and play (3) .... golf. And I'd
like to visit a museum. I really like (4) .... history.

A: (5) .... Castle Museum is really good. It's got streets and houses from a
hundred years ago. It's (6) .... interesting place.

B: Where is it?

A: It's in (7) .... Tower Street, I think. There's a nice café there, too, so you
can have (8) .... lunch there.

B: Great. Thanks for all your advice!

Check 3 Articles

1 Circle the correct answer.

1 There's *a / the* letter on the table.

2 Can I have *a / the* glass of water, please?

3 We're going to *a / the* Natural History Museum on Sunday.

4 Ben's office is on *a / the* second floor.

5 Wait! I've got *an / the* idea.

/ 5

2 Complete the extract from a letter. Use *a* or *the*.

I'm working in (6) .... shop this summer. It's (7) .... big bookshop near (8) .... town centre. I like (9) .... job because I meet a lot of people and because I can see my friends at lunchtime. There's (10) .... café in (11) .... shop, so we meet there.

/ 6

3 Choose and complete the sentences.

12 (an, the)
   I want to be .... actor.

13 (a, the)
   He plays .... guitar very well.

14 (A, The)
   .... wind's very cold.

15 (a, the)
   I'm meeting .... friend this evening.

16 (A, The)
   I've got a card and a present from Sam. .... card's very funny.

17 (a, the)
   We're staying at .... Fairview. It's a nice hotel – small and friendly.

/ 6

4 Complete the e-mail. Use *a*, *the* or −.

New Message

Dear Lisa,

We're having a great holiday. We're staying with (18) .... Blakes in (19) .... small village near (20) .... Brighton in the south of (21) .... England. (22) .... village is near (23) .... beautiful beach, so we go there every day. It's very relaxing. We have (24) .... lunch there and in the afternoon we play (25) .... tennis.

We're having a great time!
See you soon.

Love,
Sarah

/ 8

Total: / 25

✓ **Self-check**

Wrong answers	Look again at	Try CD-ROM
1, 5, 10, 11, 16, 19, 22, 23	Unit 20	Exercise 20
2, 4, 6, 8, 9, 14, 15	Unit 21	Exercise 21
3, 7, 12, 13, 17, 18, 20, 21, 24, 25	Unit 22	Exercise 22

Now do **Check 3**

Adjectives

23 small, expensive

We live in a **small** town.	Our town is **small**.
These are **expensive** shoes.	These shoes are **expensive**.

- We use adjectives to describe people or things.
- An adjective usually comes:
  - before a noun: *We live in a **small** town.*
  - after the verb *be*: *Our town is **small**.*
- An adjective does not change. It is the same for singular and plural nouns:
  *an **expensive** bag*   ***expensive** shoes*

PRACTICE

23a Put the words in the correct order.

0 I've got / mobile / a / new   *I've got a new mobile.*

1 in / live / street / quiet / we / a   ....

2 jeans / cheap / are / these   ....

3 blue / my / is / notebook   ....

4 brother / likes / my / cities / big ....

5 late / Emma and Sarah / are   ....

6 shop / they've got / small / a   ....

7 that / expensive / bag / is   ....

8 Zoe / red / loves / roses   ....

23b Circle the correct answer.

0 The beach here is (*beautiful*)/*a beautiful*.

1 The food is *delicious* /*a delicious*.

2 Emma's new car is *green* /*a green*.

3 This is *fantastic* /*a fantastic* place.

4 That bag's *heavy* /*a heavy*.

5 I've got *old* /*an old* photo of Kate here.

6 I'd like to buy *black* /*a black* T-shirt.

7 That's *great* /*a great* idea!

8 I like her. She's *nice* /*a nice*.

24 *smaller than, more expensive than*

I'm **older than** my sister Lisa. Lisa's **bigger than** me. She's **prettier than** me. She's **more intelligent than** me. But her spelling's **worse than** mine!

● We use comparative adjectives to compare two people or things.

● For short adjectives, we add *-er (than)*. Be careful of the spelling:
  old → older (than)   big → bigger (than)   pretty → prettier (than)

● For long adjectives, we use *more (than)*:
  careful → more careful (than)   intelligent → more intelligent (than)

● These comparative adjectives are irregular:
  good → better (than)   bad → worse (than)   far → farther/further (than)

▶▶ **See Appendix 2: Spelling rules for comparative and superlative adjectives, page 169.**

PRACTICE

24a Complete the sentences. Use the comparative.

   o   My brother's ....*taller*........ than me. (tall)

   1   Is Sarah .... than you? (young)

   2   Pink's a .... colour for a bedroom than orange. (pretty)

   3   My sister's got .... hair than me. (dark)

   4   Languages are .... than Science. (easy)

   5   Their house is .... than our house. (big)

   6   Don't worry about flying. Planes are .... than cars. (safe)

   7   Simon's story's .... than yours. (funny)

   8   Your idea's .... than mine. (good)

24b Complete the sentences. Use the comparative.

   o   These old buildings are ......*more attractive*...... than the modern ones. (attractive)

   1   Mountain climbing's .... than skiing. (exciting)

   2   My trainers are .... than these shoes. (comfortable)

   3   The red dress is .... than the black one. (expensive)

   4   Are computers .... than people? (intelligent)

   5   This story's .... than that one. (interesting)

   6   The second exercise is .... than the first one. (difficult)

   7   Sharks are .... than dolphins. (dangerous)

   8   Volleyball's .... than basketball at my school. (popular)

24C **Read about the two swimming pools and complete the sentences. Use the comparative.**

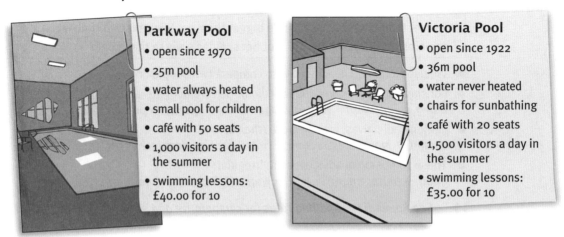

Parkway Pool
- open since 1970
- 25m pool
- water always heated
- small pool for children
- café with 50 seats
- 1,000 visitors a day in the summer
- swimming lessons: £40.00 for 10

Victoria Pool
- open since 1922
- 36m pool
- water never heated
- chairs for sunbathing
- café with 20 seats
- 1,500 visitors a day in the summer
- swimming lessons: £35.00 for 10

0 ......*Victoria*...... Pool is ......*older than Parkway*...... Pool. (old)

1 .... Pool is .... Pool. (long)

2 .... Pool is .... Pool! (cold)

3 .... Pool is .... for children. (good)

4 The café at .... Pool is .... the café at .... Pool. (big)

5 .... Pool is .... Pool in the summer. (crowded)

6 The lessons at .... Pool are .... the lessons at .... Pool. (expensive)

25 *the smallest, the most expensive*

> This is **the smallest** TV in the shop. That's **the biggest** – and the **most expensive**.
> This is **the best** DVD player.

- We use superlative adjectives to compare a person or thing with a number of other people or things.
- For short adjectives, we add *the + -est*. Be careful of the spelling:
  small → **the** small**est**   big → **the** big**gest**   happy → **the** happ**iest**
- For long adjectives, we use *the most*:
  expensive → **the most** expensive   popular → **the most** popular
- These superlative adjectives are irregular:
  good → the best   bad → the worst   far → the farthest/furthest

▶▶ **See Appendix 2: Spelling rules for comparative and superlative adjectives, page 169.**

P R A C T I C E

25a Complete the conversations. Use the superlative.

0 **A:** Have you got a water bottle for the walking trip next week?
   B: Yes – this one. It isn't very big, but it's .... *the lightest* .... (light)

1 **A:** I'm looking for some cheap sunglasses.
   B: These are .... sunglasses. They're £14.99. (cheap)

2 **A:** Is that puzzle good?
   B: Yes. It's .... puzzle in the book! (difficult)

3 **A:** Do you like these T-shirts?
   B: Yes. .... one is that blue one. (pretty)

4 **A:** Have you got any books about the *Star Wars* films?
   B: Yes, we've got these three. That's .... one – *A Guide to Star Wars*. (interesting)

5 **A:** Where can I get some good pencils for my art class?
   B: .... art shop is Smith's in Green Street. (good)

6 **A:** What's your favourite programme?
   B: *The Simpsons*. It's .... programme on TV. (funny)

7 **A:** Do you want to get an ice cream?
   B: Yes, OK. This Italian shop sells .... ones – and they're fantastic! (big)

8 **A:** I love that dress!
   B: Yes, it's beautiful. But it's .... dress in the shop! (expensive)

25b Complete the sentences. Use the superlative.

dangerous	deep	expensive	far	high	~~large~~	long	old	sunny

0 The Sahara is .... *the largest* .... desert in the world.

1 .... pyramid in the world is over 4,500 years old.

2 Mount Everest is .... mountain in the world.

3 Yuma in Arizona is .... city in the world. It has about 4,000 hours of sunshine every year.

4 Lake Baikal in Siberia is .... lake in the world. It is about 1600 metres deep.

5 The Nile is .... river. It reaches the sea after a journey of 6,695 kilometres.

6 Mauritius is .... country for road accidents.

7 Neptune is .... planet from the sun.

8 Tokyo is .... city in Japan. You need a lot of money to live there.

26 *smaller than, the smallest*

Comparative	Superlative
Your mobile's **smaller than** mine.	This mobile is **the smallest** in the shop.
Your camera's **more expensive than** mine.	This camera is **the most expensive** in the shop.

▶▶ **See Units 24–25.**

P R A C T I C E

26a Look at the pictures and complete the sentences. Use the comparative or superlative.

Beth   Lucy   Rachel

0 (short, tall)

    a Lucy is ....*shorter than*.... Beth.

    b Beth is ....*the tallest*.... .

    c Rachel is ....*the shortest*.... .

1 (cold, warm)

    a Monday will be .... Tuesday.

    b Tuesday will be .... day.

    c Friday will be .... day.

2 (boring, interesting)

    a The first book is .... the second book.

    b The second book is ....

    c The third book is ....

26b Complete the conversation. Use the comparative or superlative.

    A: Where do you go to the cinema?

    B: I usually go to CineLand. It's (0) ....*the nearest*.... (near) cinema to my house.

    A: Is it (1) .... (cheap) MovieWorld?

    B: No, but it's (2) .... (nice). The seats are (3) .... (comfortable).

    A: Do you sometimes go to City Cinema?

    B: No, never! That's (4) .... (bad) in town! Do you go there?

    A: No, I go to MovieWorld. It has (5) .... (good) films, I think. They aren't always (6) .... (popular), but they're interesting.

27 *a nice blue shirt*

Tom's wearing a **nice blue** shirt.   There are some **large yellow** flowers in that vase.

When there is more than one adjective before a noun, we use this order:

	Opinion	Size	Colour	
a	**nice**		**blue**	shirt
some		**large**	**yellow**	flowers
a	**beautiful**	**big**		bag

P R A C T I C E

27a Put the words in the correct order.

0 tree / tall / a / beautiful   *a beautiful tall tree* ....

1 a / garden / lovely / big   ....

2 pink / a / T-shirt / pretty   ....

3 awful / some / trousers / orange   ....

4 cat / a / black / small   ....

5 beach / beautiful / white / a   ....

6 green / big / bags / some   ....

27b Put the adjectives in the correct order.

A: Have you got any (0) ....*long white*........ (long, white) skirts?

B: No. We've only got (1) .... (white, short) ones.

A: What are you going to buy?

B: Some (2) .... (green, big) apples and some

(3) .... (nice, red) grapes.

A: There are some great things in this shop!

B: Oh – what?

A: There are some (4) .... (amazing, little) watches and

some (5) .... (big, beautiful) clocks.

A: Can you see any (6) .... (black, nice) jackets?

B: There are some (7) .... (short, nice) ones over there.

A: What kind of sandals are you looking for?

B: Some (8) .... (pretty, blue) ones. I want to wear

them with a (9) .... (blue, long) dress.

A: We've got these (10) .... (blue, lovely) ones.

B: Hmm ... I'm not sure they're the right colour.

Adverbs

28 *slow, slowly*

I'm a **slow** reader.	I read **slowly**.
Kirsty's a **good** singer.	Kirsty sings **well**.
Sam's a **fast** runner.	Sam runs **fast**.

- We use adjectives to describe people or things: *I'm a **slow** reader.*
- We use adverbs to describe how someone or something does something: *I read **slowly**.*
- To make an adverb, we usually add *-ly* at the end of an adjective. Be careful of spelling changes: *slow → slowly   angry → angrily*
- This adverb is irregular: *good → well*
- These words can be both adjectives and adverbs. They do not change: *fast → fast   hard → hard*

▶▶ **See Appendix 3: Spelling rules for adverbs, page 169.**

⚠️ Adverbs of manner usually come:
  - after the verb: *Kirsty sings **well**.*
  - after the verb and object: *He learns everything **quickly**.*

PRACTICE

28a Complete the sentences. Use adverbs.

0 They're all smiling ..... *happily* ..... . (happy)

1 Hurry up! Don't walk so .... (slow)

2 He always explains things .... (clear)

3 The children are playing .... in the pool. (noisy)

4 Ben makes friends .... (easy)

5 Don't eat so .... (quick)

6 You speak German .... (perfect)

7 Helen always talks .... (loud)

8 Please listen .... (careful)

9 Rob sometimes laughs .... (nervous)

10 Harry's looking at Clare .... (angry)

28b Re-write the sentences. Use adverbs.

o	He's a beautiful singer.	*He sings beautifully.* ....
1	She's a bad player.	....
2	He's a dangerous driver.	....
3	They're hard workers.	....
4	I'm a fast learner.	....
5	You're a good writer.	....
6	She's a wonderful dancer.	....

28c Circle the correct answer.

A: Hi, Sophie. Where are you?

B: I'm in the car with Aisha. We're going to town, but the traffic's very bad. We're moving very (o) *slow /(slowly)*. Where are you?

A: I'm in town with Rachel. It's very (1) *busy /busily*. We're in a (2) *brilliant / brilliantly* shop, and I'm looking at some (3) *beautiful / beautifully* earrings.

B: Why are you (4) *sudden /suddenly* talking (5) *quiet /quietly*?

A: Because I want to buy them for Rachel. It's her birthday on Tuesday.

B: Your presents are always (6) *nice /nicely*. You choose them very (7) *careful /carefully*.

A: Thanks! What time will you be here, do you think?

B: Um ... at about three, I think.

A: OK. See you soon. Drive (8) *safe /safely*.

29 *more slowly, the most slowly*

> Emma eats **more slowly than** me. Of all the people in our family, Emma eats **the most slowly**.
>
> Tom works **harder than** Rob. Of all the students in my class, Tom works **the hardest**.

- To form the comparative and superlative of adverbs:
  - We add *more* or *the most* before adverbs ending in *-ly*:
    slowly → **more** *slowly* → **the most** *slowly*
  - We add *-er (than)* or *the -est* to one-syllable adverbs:
    hard → *hard**er*** → **the** *hard**est***
- The comparative and superlative forms of these adverbs are different:
  well → *better* → *the best*   *badly* → *worse* → *the worst*

P R A C T I C E

29a **Complete the sentences. Use the comparative or superlative.**

o You can remember people .... *better than* .... I can. (well)

1 Kim, Kate and Jo all sing well, but Kate sings ....
(beautifully)

2 Stuart explains things .... Nick. (clearly)

3 Of all drivers, young people drive .... (dangerously)

4 My friends and I don't eat well, but Vicky eats .... of
all of us. (badly)

5 Emma works .... Nikki. (hard)

6 James can run .... his brother. (fast)

29b **Nicole and her friends are going on a camping trip. They need a leader for their group. Look at the table and complete the sentences. Use the comparative or superlative. Who would be the best leader?**

	Nicole	Jamie	Anna	Robert	Philip
reads maps easily	•••	••	•	•••	••••
cooks well	•	•••	••••	•••	••
thinks fast	••	••	••	•••	••••
listens to people carefully	••••	••	••	•••	•
decides things calmly	•••	••	••	••••	••

o Nicole reads maps .... *more easily than* .... Jamie and Anna.

1 Philip reads maps ....

2 Robert reads maps .... Jamie and Anna.

3 Jamie cooks .... Philip and Nicole.

4 Anna cooks ....

5 Robert thinks .... Nicole, Jamie and Anna.

6 Philip thinks ....

7 Robert listens to people .... Jamie, Anna and Philip.

8 Nicole listens to people ....

9 Nicole decides things .... Jamie, Anna and Philip.

10 Robert decides things ....

.... would be the best leader.

30 *too small, not big enough*

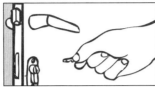

*The key is **too** small.*

*The box is**n't** big **enough**.*

- *Too* means 'more than you need'.
- *Not ... enough* means 'less than you need'.

P R A C T I C E

30a Write sentences. Use *too* and the words in brackets.

o I can't wear these shoes. ..*They're too big.*............. (they / big)

1 I can't buy these trainers. .... (they / expensive)

2 I don't like cola. .... (it / sweet)

3 I don't want to wear this dress. .... (it / long)

4 I can't do this now. .... (I / tired)

5 Lucy can't come with us. .... (she / busy)

30b Complete the sentences. Use *not ... enough* and the adjectives in brackets.

o I never hear my mobile phone. The ring ....*isn't loud enough*............. . (loud)

1 I won't pass my driving test. I .... (good)

2 I can never do these crosswords. I .... ! (clever)

3 Don't use that computer. It .... (fast)

4 Sarah wants to be a model but she .... (tall)

5 That restaurant's nice but it .... (big)

30c Circle the correct answer.

o I can't move this desk. I'm *too strong* / (*not strong enough*).

1 She can't reach the top shelf. She's *too short* / *not short enough*.

2 He can't ask her out. He's *too shy* / *not shy enough*.

3 You can't vote because you're not eighteen. You're *too old* / *not old enough*.

4 I can't go skiing. I'm *too fit* / *not fit enough*.

5 I can't do this exercise! It's *too difficult* / *not difficult enough*!

6 My coffee's *too strong* / *not strong enough*. I need more caffeine!

31 *always, never*

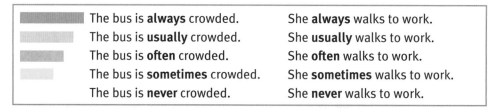

	The bus is **always** crowded.	She **always** walks to work.
	The bus is **usually** crowded.	She **usually** walks to work.
	The bus is **often** crowded.	She **often** walks to work.
	The bus is **sometimes** crowded.	She **sometimes** walks to work.
	The bus is **never** crowded.	She **never** walks to work.

● We use adverbs of frequency to describe how often somebody does something, or how often something happens.

● Adverbs of frequency come after the verb *be*: *The bus **is always** crowded.*

● And they come before other verbs: *She **sometimes walks** to work.*

● In negative sentences, they come between *don' t/doesn' t* and the verb: *I **don't usually buy** magazines.*

● In questions, they come before the verb: *Do you **always have** breakfast?*

 We can use *every* + noun, too (e.g. *every day, every week, every year*). *Every day/week*, etc. come at the beginning or end of the sentence: *I phone Emma **every day**.* ***Every month** we visit my grandparents.*

PRACTICE

31a Re-write the sentences. Put the adverbs in the correct place.

0 I watch TV in the evening. (often)
I often watch TV in the evening.
....

1 Joe and I go swimming. (sometimes)
....

2 Our street is quiet. (always)
....

3 My father plays football with me. (sometimes)
....

4 We go to the beach. (often)
....

5 My brother gets up at six. (usually)
....

6 I drink coffee. (never)
....

7 Our holidays in Spain are wonderful. (always)
....

8 Jason goes to bed at nine. (usually)
....

31b **Put the words in the correct order.**

0 you / do / sometimes/ to town / walk?
Do you sometimes walk to town?
....

1 don't / my friends / go home / usually / on the bus
....

2 Ashley / phone / does / sometimes / you?
....

3 expensive / aren't / usually / the tickets
....

4 on Saturdays / doesn't / work / my mum / often
....

5 your sister / is / funny / always?
....

6 you / on Saturdays / always / do / go out?
....

7 often / isn't / the train / crowded
....

8 they / often / their cousins / do / visit?
....

31c **Look at the table and write sentences about Kelly and her brother Mark.**

	Kelly	**Mark**
do homework	always	usually
write for the school magazine	not often	every month
do karate	every week	never
play the piano	never	every day
be ill	often	not often

0 Kelly / do homework .... *Kelly always does her homework.*

1 Kelly / write for the school magazine ....

2 Mark / write for the school magazine ....

3 Kelly / do karate ....

4 Mark / do karate ....

5 Kelly / play the piano ....

6 Mark / play the piano ....

7 Kelly / be ill ....

8 Mark / be ill ....

Check 4 Adjectives and adverbs

1 Put the words in the correct order.

1 London / I / go / sometimes / to

....

2 awful / programme / is / this

....

3 Luke / late / is / never

....

4 always / dinner at eight / have / we

....

5 dark / hair / long / has got / Kate

....

/ 5

2 Circle the correct answer.

A: These shoes (6) *are too small / aren't small enough*. I need some bigger ones.

B: Are they (7) *more / the most* expensive than the brown ones?

A: Yes. They're £40. Hmm ... they hurt a bit. (8) They*'re too wide / aren't wide enough* here. I've got (9) *wide feet / feet wide*.

B: What about these (10) *little black / black little* ones?

/ 5

3 Complete the sentences. Use the words in the box. You do not need all of them.

> beautiful beautifully careful
> carefully loud loudly

11 She's very .... with her violin because it's expensive.

12 Mark always laughs .... at my jokes.

13 I always read instructions very

....

14 I don't like .... noises.

15 She's got an amazing voice. She sings

....

/ 5

4 Complete the conversations. Use the comparative or superlative.

16 A: Does your sister cycle to school with you?

B: No. She never cycles or walks. She's .... person in the world! (lazy)

17 A: Do you like swimming?

B: No. I'm .... swimmer in my class! (bad)

18 A: Anna's very good at tennis.

B: Yes. She plays .... than her sister. (well)

19 A: I like Biology but I don't like Physics.

B: I think Physics is .... than Biology. (interesting)

20 A: Emma always gets the highest marks in music exams.

B: I know. She works .... in the class. She practises for hours every day. (hard)

/ 5

Total: / 20

Self-check

Wrong answers	Look again at	Try CD-ROM
2, 9	Unit 23	Exercise 23
7, 16, 17, 19	Units 24–26	Exercises 24-26
5, 10	Unit 27	Exercise 27
11, 12, 13, 14, 15	Unit 28	Exercise 28
18, 20	Unit 29	Exercise 29
6, 8	Unit 30	Exercise 30
1, 3, 4	Unit 31	Exercise 31

Now do **Check 4**

Present tenses

32 *I'm Sam.*

I'**m** Sam.   He **isn't** ready.   **Are** they here?

We use *be*:

- to say who somebody is or what something is: *I'**m** Sam.   That'**s** my ticket.*
- to describe something or somebody: *Your shoes **are** nice.   He'**s** tall.*
- to say where somebody is from: *He'**s** American.   We'**re** from Brazil.*
- to talk about people's jobs: *She'**s** a teacher.   My father'**s** a doctor.*
- to talk about somebody's age: *I'**m** nineteen.   Sally'**s** twenty one.*
- to say how we feel: *We'**re** tired.   He'**s** angry.*
- to say where somebody or something is: *She'**s** at home.   Your bag'**s** on the chair.*
- to talk about somebody's health: *I'**m** fine.   Kate'**s** ill.*

Affirmative	Negative	Question
I'**m (am)**	I'**m not (am not)**	**Am** I?
he/she/it'**s (is)**	he/she/it **isn't (is not)**	**Is** he/she/it?
you/we/they'**re (are)**	you/we/they **aren't (are not)**	**Are** you/we/they?

Short answers	Yes, I **am.**	Yes, he/she/it **is.**	Yes, you/we/they **are.**
	No, I'**m not.**	No, he/she/it **isn't.**	No, you/we/they **aren't.**

▶▶ **See Appendix 11: Short forms of verbs, page 171.**

P R A C T I C E

32a Complete what Richard says. Use *am*, *is* or *are*.

My name (0) ......*is*...... Richard. I (1) ...am........ twenty one. I (2) ...am........
a student at Bristol University. Bristol (3) ...is........... a big city in the west of
England. My parents (4) ...are....... from Nigeria but I (5) ...am........ British. My
two brothers (6) ...are...... lawyers and my sister (7) ...is........... an accountant.
My brothers and sister (8) ...are...... married but I (9) ...am..... single.
I have a niece, too. She (10) ...is........... three.

32b Correct the sentences. Use the short forms of *be*.

0 A: She's Japanese. (Korean) B: No, *she isn't Japanese. She's Korean* .

1 A: We're late. (early) B: No, we aren't late we're late

2 A: They're from Italy. (Poland) B: No, They aren't from italy. They ar

3 A: You're ill. (fine) B: No, you aren't ill you are fine .

4 A: He's a journalist. (doctor) B: No, He isn't a journalist. He is doctor

5 A: I'm fat. (thin) B: No, I am not fatus I'm thin .

32c Complete the conversation. Use *be* and the words in brackets.

A: (0) *Are you and Teri* (you and Teri) in the same band?

B: No, (00) *we aren't* .

A: (1) Are you (you) the singer in your band?

B: No, (2) I'm not . I'm the drummer.

A: (3) is Kim (Kim) the singer?

B: Yes. And Laura's the guitarist.

A: Really? (4) are they (Laura and Kim) sisters?

B: No, (5) They aren't . They're friends.

A: Oh. So, (6) Is your gig (your gig) on Saturday at the KoolKlub?

B: No, (7) I am not . it isn't

A: Where (8) is (it)?

B: It's at the T8, at 9.30.

A: And (9) are you (you) ready for it?

B: Yes, (10) I'm .

A: Good luck then!

B: Thanks.

32d Complete the e-mail. Use *be*.

New Message

Hi, Alex!

How (0) ...are... you? How (1) ...is... Nikki? I (2) ...am... fine. My hostel (3) ..is........ OK. My room (4) isn't big, but it's comfortable. Sarah and Neil (5) ....are... in London this year, too. They (6) ...aren't... on my course, but they're at my college, and Sarah and I (7) ...are... in the same hostel.

What about you? (8) ....is... your new job interesting? Do you like it?

Write soon!

Clare

33 I've got a computer.

from Poland

| I've got a computer. | They haven't got a car. | Has he got dark hair? |

We use *have got*:

- to talk about possession: *I've got a computer.*   *They **haven't got** a car.*
- to describe somebody: *She's got blue eyes.*   ***Has** he **got** dark hair?*
- to talk about illnesses: *I've got a headache.*   ***Have** you **got** a cold?*

Affirmative	I/you/we/they've got (have got)	he/she it's got (has got)
Negative	I/you/we/they haven't got (have not got)	he/she/it hasn't got (has not got)
Question	Have I/you/we/they got?	Has he/she/it got?
Short answers	Yes, I/you/we/they have.	Yes, he/she/it has.
	No, I/you/we/they haven't.	No, he/she/it hasn't.

▶▶ ***See Appendix 11: Short forms of verbs, page 171.***

⚠ We can use *have* instead of *have got*:
*She **has** blue eyes.*   *They **don't have** a car.*   ***Do** you **have** a cold?*
But *have got* is more common in British English.

▶▶ ***For the forms of verbs in the present simple, see Units 34–36.***

P R A C T I C E

33a Write sentences. Use *have got* and the words in brackets.

   0 A: Have you got a motorbike? B: No. *I've got a car.* .... (I / a car)

   1 A: Have you got a hairbrush? B: No. .... (I / a comb)

   2 A: Has Kirsty got dark hair? B: No. .... (she / fair hair)

   3 A: Why is he in bed? B: .... (he / a cold)

   4 A: Where are the sandwiches? B: .... (we / them)

   5 A: Are you all right? B: No. .... (I / a headache)

   6 A: Has Lisa got a brother? B: No. .... (she / a sister)

   7 A: Have they got any pets? B: .... (they / a cat)

   8 A: Have you got any money? B: .... (we / £50)

   9 A: Have they got any children? B: .... (they / a little boy)

 10 A: Has your town got a theatre? B: No. .... (it / a cinema)

33b **Look at the table and complete the sentences. Use *have got*.**

	flat	house	garden	car	dog
Tanya	✓	✗	✗	✓	✗
Kim and Dave	✗	✓	✓	✗	✓
Matt and I	✓	✗	✗	✓	✗

o Tanya ....*'s got*........ a flat. She ....*hasn't got*........ a house or a garden.

1 She .... a car. She .... a dog.

2 Kim and Dave .... a flat. They .... a house and a garden.

3 They .... a car. They .... a dog.

4 Matt and I .... a flat. We .... a house or a garden.

5 We .... a car. We .... a dog.

33c **Write questions. Use *have got*.**

o she / long hair?   *Has she got long hair?* ....

1 you / a headache? ....

2 your brother / a bike? ....

3 they / a computer? ....

4 Emma / brown eyes? ....

5 he / a cold? ....

6 Mick and Anna / a car? ....

33d **Complete the conversations. Use *have got*.**

A: (0) ...*Have*... you ...*got*... a cold?

B: Yes. And I (1) .... a terrible headache. (2) .... you .... any aspirin?

A: No, I (3) .... Sorry. (4) .... Lucy .... any?

B: I don't know. Maybe.

A: (5) .... Emma and Isabel .... the information about the trip?

B: Yes, they (6) .... But they (7) .... the tickets.

A: Don't worry. Daniel (8) .... them.

A: (9) .... your car .... a CD player?

B: No, it (10) .... It (11) .... a radio and a cassette player. I (12) .... any cassettes, I'm afraid.

A: That's OK. We can listen to the radio.

34 *I live here.*

I **live** here.   She often **phones** me.   They **play** football every day.

- We use the present simple:
  - to talk about something that is always or usually true:
    *I **live** here.   Children **ask** a lot of questions.*
  - to talk about things that happen regularly:
    *She often **phones** me.   They **play** football every day.*
- We often use adverbs of frequency (e.g. *always, usually, often, sometimes, never*) and other time expressions (e.g. *every day, in the morning*) with the present simple. The adverbs come before the verb. *Every day, in the morning,* etc. come at the beginning or end of the sentence:
  *She **often** phones me.   They play football **every day**.*
- In affirmative sentences, we add *-s* or *-es* in the third person singular (*he, she, it*):
  *I live → he live**s**   we watch → she watch**es**   they fly → it fli**es***

Affirmative	I/you/we/they **live** he/she/it **lives**

▶▶ **See Appendix 4: Spelling rules for present simple verbs (he/she/it), page 169.**

▶▶ **For adverbs of frequency, see Unit 31.**

P R A C T I C E

34a Complete the table.

I/you/we/they	he/she/it	I/you/we/they	he/she/it
finish	*finishes*	stay	
teach		study	
try		give	
like		say	
wash		mix	
worry		wear	
go		touch	
miss		listen	
start		cry	
carry		live	
lie		want	

34b **Circle the correct answer.**

We're English but we (0) *live* /lives in France. I (1) *go* /goes to university and my brother (2) go /*goes* to school here. I (3) *like* /likes France, but I (4) *miss* /misses my friends in England. They (5) *write* /writes to me, and sometimes they (6) *visit* /visits. My friend Emily always (7) come /*comes* here in the summer. We always (8) *have* /has a great time together.

34c **Complete the extract from a magazine article. Use the present simple of the verbs in brackets.**

In Britain, when couples get married, they usually (0) ....*invite*........ (invite) their family and friends to the wedding. The bride's father (1) .... (bring) the bride to the ceremony. She usually (2) .... (wear) a white dress. The 'best man' (3) .... (help) the groom before and at the wedding. Usually, he is a very good friend of the groom.

After the ceremony, there is a special meal and a party. At the end of the meal, the bride and groom (4) .... (cut) their wedding cake together and all the guests (5) .... (get) a piece. After the party, the bride and groom (6) .... (go) on their honeymoon.

34d **Put the words in the correct order.**

0 Kate / gets up / usually / early   *Kate usually gets up early.*

1 often / clothes / my friends / buy   ....

2 never / forget / I / my friends' birthdays   ....

3 every morning / coffee / Clare / drinks   ....

4 they / have lunch / at 12.00 / always   ....

5 we / to the cinema / every week / go   ....

34e **How often do you do these things? Write sentences that are true for you. Use the present simple.**

0 (get up early)   *I always/usually/often/never get up early.*

1 (buy clothes)   ....

2 (forget friends' birthdays)   ....

3 (drink coffee)   ....

4 (have lunch at 12.00)   ....

5 (go to the cinema)   ....

35 *I don't live here.*

I **don't live** here. He **doesn't drive**. We **don't play** chess.

Negative	I/you/we/they **don't (do not) live**
	he/she/it **doesn't (does not) live**

⚠ There is no *-s* at the end of the verb in the third person singular:
He doesn't drive. (Not *He doesn't drives.*)

▶▶ *See Appendix 11: Short forms of verbs, page 171.*

PRACTICE

35a Circle the correct answer.

0 We (*don't play*)/*doesn't play* football every day.

1 He *don't live* /*doesn't live* in Cambridge.

2 The shop *don't open* /*doesn't open* on Saturdays.

3 I *don't go* /*doesn't go* to college on Tuesdays.

4 My mum *don't like* /*doesn't like* rap music.

5 You *don't know* /*doesn't know* her.

6 They *don't sell* /*doesn't sell* newspapers.

7 We *don't visit* /*doesn't visit* them every week.

8 Josh and Tom *don't do* /*doesn't do* much at weekends.

35b Complete the sentences. Use the present simple of the verbs in brackets.

0 I sometimes play volleyball. I .... *don't do* .... a lot of exercise. (not do)

1 My brothers watch a lot of television. They .... any newspapers or magazines. (not read)

2 My sister cycles to college. She .... (not walk)

3 My parents stay at home on Sundays. They .... (not go out)

4 My uncle works very hard, but he .... the money. (not need)

5 Alice lives in Milan, but she .... Italian. (not speak)

6 I like tea. I .... a lot of coffee. (not drink)

7 Of course we like parties! But we .... to go out tonight. (not want)

8 I understand the question, but I .... the answer. (not know)

35c **Complete Anna's letter to a magazine. Use the present simple of the verbs in the box.**

| not know | ~~not like~~ | not say | not talk | not understand | not want |

I'm not happy at my new college. The people in my class (0) ....*don't like*...... me. I (1) ....?............... the lessons. I think my brother knows, but he (2) .... anything. We (3) .... about our problems.

I often talk to my friends on the Internet about it. They help me a lot. They (4) .... my real name, so I can tell them everything. I (5) .... to tell my parents about it, but they know I'm not happy.

What's your advice?

Anna

36 *Do you live here?*

| **Do** you **live** here? | **Does** he **speak** German? | What **do** they **want**? |

Question	**Do** I/you/we/they **live**?	**Does** he/she/it **live**?
Short **answers**	Yes, I/you/we/they **do**.	Yes, he/she/it **does**.
	No, I/you/we/they **don't**.	No, he/she/it **doesn't**.

There is no *-s* at the end of the verb in the third person singular: *Does he speak German?* (Not *Does he speaks German?*)

▶▶ *For questions with 'what', 'where', 'when', etc., see Units 73–74.*

P R A C T I C E

36a **Write questions. Use the present simple.**

0 you / like / this song? *Do you like this song?* ....

1 that shop / sell / cold drinks? ....

2 where / your sister / work? ....

3 they / play / rock music? ....

4 we / need / any sugar? ....

5 when / he / play / football? ....

6 what / you / want? ....

36b **Complete the short answers.**

    0   **A:** Do you speak Arabic?   **B:** Yes, *I do* ....

    1   **A:** Do your parents come from Egypt?   **B:** No, ...

    2   **A:** Do you live in Jordan?   **B:** No, ...

    3   **A:** Does your brother live in Canada, too?   **B:** No, ...

    4   **A:** Does he live in Jordan?   **B:** Yes, ...

    5   **A:** Does he often visit you in Canada?   **B:** No, ...

    6   **A:** Do you visit him?   **B:** Yes, ...

36c **Write short answers that are true for you.**

    0   Do you play a musical instrument?   *Yes, I do. / No, I don't.*

    1   Do you drive?   ....

    2   Do you work?   ....

    3   Do you do any sport?   ....

    4   Do you like rock music?   ....

    5   Do you drink a lot of coffee?   ....

    6   Do you travel a lot?   ....

36d **Jamie is with his friends Rob and Lisa. Lisa's friend Tessa is with them. Read Tessa's answers and write Jamie's questions. Use the phrases in the box.**

when / you / play	you and Lisa / play / tennis together
where / you / live	~~you / know / Lisa from college~~
your dad / wear / glasses	your parents / have / a blue Audi

Jamie: (0) *Do you know Lisa from college?* ....

Tessa: No, I don't. We're neighbours.

Jamie: (1) ....

Tessa: In East Street – I live next door to Lisa.

Jamie: (2) ....

Tessa: Yes, they do. It's usually outside the house.

Jamie: (3) ....

Tessa: Yes, he does. And he's got dark hair.

Jamie: (4) ....

Tessa: No, we don't. We play badminton.

Jamie: (5) ....

Tessa: On Mondays and Wednesdays. Sometimes we play on Fridays, too.

Check 5 Present simple

1 **Complete the sentences. Use the correct form of *be* or *have got*.**

1 They .... Chinese. They're from America.

2 This is my sister. Her name .... Vicki.

3 He .... a car, but he's got a motorbike.

4 No, I don't work. I .... a student.

5 We .... some bread and cheese. Would you like a sandwich?

6 Sarah can't come with us. She .... busy.

7 They .... a small house in the country. It's lovely.

/ 7

2 **Put the words in the correct order.**

8 is / your name / what?

....

9 you / a map / have / got?

....

10 often / we / to the park / go

....

11 wear / doesn't / he / glasses

....

12 they / where / live / do?

....

13 tennis / Rob / play / doesn't

....

14 don't / coffee / I / drink

....

/ 7

3 **Complete what Kelly says. Use the present simple of the verbs in brackets.**

My friend Hannah and I sometimes (15) .... (go) to the beach on Sundays. We usually (16) .... (cycle) there. My sister (17) .... (not come) with us because she (18) .... (not like) the sea. She (19) .... (prefer) the city.

/ 5

4 **Complete the conversations. Use one word in each gap.**

20 A: Why .... Mick need £1,000?
   B: He wants to buy a new computer.

21 A: Does Kate's cousin work here?
   B: Yes, she ....

22 A: How many CDs .... he got?
   B: A lot!

23 A: .... you do a lot of sport?
   B: No, I don't.

24 A: Do you visit them every week?
   B: Yes, we ....

25 A: How much money .... you got?
   B: £50.

/ 6

Total: / 25

✓ Self-check

Wrong answers	Look again at	Try CD-ROM
1, 2, 4, 6, 8	Unit 32	Exercise 32
3, 5, 7, 9, 22, 25	Unit 33	Exercise 33
10, 15, 16, 19	Unit 34	Exercise 34
11, 13, 14, 17, 18	Unit 35	Exercise 35
12, 20, 21, 23, 24	Unit 36	Exercise 36

Now do **Check 5**

37 *I'm going home.*

> I'm **going** home.   She**'s** work**ing**.   They**'re** swim**ming**.

We use the present continuous to talk about something that is happening now, at exactly this moment. We often use it with time words and phrases like *now*, *right now* or *at the moment*: *She's working at the moment.*

Affirmative		
I'm **(am)** go**ing**	he/she/it**'s (is)** go**ing**	you/we/they**'re (are)** go**ing**

▶▶   **See Appendix 5: Spelling rules for verbs + -ing, page 170.**

▶▶   **See Appendix 11: Short forms of verbs, page 171.**

PRACTICE

37a Complete the table.

Infinitive	-*ing* form	Infinitive	-*ing* form
stop	*stopping*	lie	
get		win	
smile		make	
ask		wear	
drive		ride	
dream		watch	
hit		jump	
shut		drink	

37b Complete the sentences. Use the present continuous of the verbs in brackets.

0 We ......*'re having*........ a party on the beach. (have)

1 Some people .... some food over a fire. (cook)

2 Ed .... the guitar. (play)

3 Joanna .... (sing)

4 A few people .... (dance)

5 Jack and Louise .... (swim)

6 Some people .... near the fire. (sit)

7 Matt .... a story. (tell)

8 Nikki and Kirsty .... to him. (listen)

9 Leah .... photos. (take)

10 Matt's dog .... up and down the beach. (run)

37c **Look at the pictures and write sentences in the present continuous. Use the phrases in the box.**

| have / breakfast | lie / on the grass | play / volleyball |
| read / a newspaper | watch / a DVD | write / a postcard |

0 *He's reading a newspaper.* ....

1 ....

2 ....

3 ....

4 ....

5 ....

37d **Complete the conversation. Use the present continuous of the verbs in brackets.**

Hannah: Hi, Simon. It's me, Hannah.

Simon: Hi. Where are you?

Hannah: In town. I (0) ....*'m having*...... (have) lunch with Emma and Luke.

Simon: Oh, can I say hi to them?

Hannah: No, not really. Emma (1) .... (talk) to Rosie on the phone and Luke (2) .... (order) our food. What's that noise?

Simon: My parents (3) .... (move) the furniture because they want to paint the living room. They (4) .... (put) all the furniture in the garden!

Hannah: Oh. Do you want to meet us here? What are you doing?

Simon: I (5) .... (listen) to my new CD. Yes, I can come. Where are you?

Hannah: We're at the Green Food Café. We (6) .... (sit) upstairs, by the window.

Simon: OK. See you in half an hour!

38 She isn't going home. / Is he sleeping?

| I'm not talking to you. | She isn't going home. | They aren't working. |
| Am I driving too fast? | Is he sleeping? | What are they doing? |

Negative		
I'm not (am not) going	he/she/it isn't (is not) going	you/we/they aren't (are not) going
Question		
Am I going?	Is he/she/it going?	Are you/we/they going?
Short answers		
Yes, I am.	Yes, he/she/it is.	Yes, you/we/they are.
No, I'm not.	No, he/she/it isn't.	No, you/we/they aren't.

▶▶ **See Appendix 11: Short forms of verbs, page 171.**

P R A C T I C E

38a Complete the sentences. Use the present continuous of the verbs in brackets.

0 Ryan isn't busy. He ....*isn't doing*........ anything. (not do)

1 You're very quiet. You .... to anyone. (not talk)

2 We're in a hotel. We .... with our cousins. (not stay)

3 Kirsty .... her glasses. (not wear)

4 I .... this programme. Let's watch something else. (not enjoy)

5 They want to go home. They .... a good time. (not have)

6 Luke .... He's in bed. (not work)

38b Write questions. Use the present continuous.

0 they / wait / for us?   *Are they waiting for us?*

1 Adam / use / his laptop?   ....

2 where / you / go?   ....

3 why / Kate and Lisa / laugh? ....

4 I / sit / in your chair?   ....

5 it / rain?   ....

6 why / he / look / at me?   ....

7 Emma / work?   ....

8 why / you / wear / my sunglasses? ....

38c **Write questions. Then complete the short answers. Use the present continuous.**

0 (you / work / on your project?)
A: *Are you working on your project?*
B: No, *I'm not* .

1 (you / watch / TV?)
A: Are you watching tv?
B: Yes, you are .

2 (Rob / watch / with you?)
A: Is Rob with you
B: No, isn't . He's out. He's at the sports centre with Philip.

3 (they / play / tennis?)
A: Are the playing tennis
B: No, they aren't .

4 (they / train / for their race?)
A: ....
B: Yes, ...

5 (Sam and Tim / train / with them?)
A: ....
B: No, ... Sam's ill and Tim's busy.

6 (he / revise / for his exams?)
A: ....
B: Yes, ... They start next week.

38d **Complete the conversation. Use the present continuous of the verbs in brackets.**

Kate: Hi, Becky. It's Kate.
Becky: Oh, hi, Kate.
Kate: Are you busy?
Becky: Well, I'm cleaning my room. What about you? (o) ....*Are you coming*....
(you / come) home?
Kate: Yes, (1) .... Well, I'm on a bus but it (2) ....
(not move)! I'm in a big traffic jam. There are some policemen here, but
they (3) .... (not do) anything. It's very annoying! What's
that music? What (4) .... (Jack / do)?
(5) .... (he / play) the guitar again?
Becky: No, (6) .... It's his friend, Scott. He's playing the banjo!
Kate: It's nice. Oh, the bus is going now! See you soon. Bye.
Becky: Bye.

39 *he goes / he's going*

Compare the present simple and present continuous:

He **goes** to the beach **every Sunday**.

He**'s going** to the cinema **now**.

⚠️ We usually use these verbs (state verbs) in the present simple – not in the present continuous: *believe, hate, know, like, love, need, remember, understand, want: I **don't understand**.* (Not ~~I'm not understanding~~.)

▶▶ **For a list of some common state verbs, see Appendix 8, page 170.**

PRACTICE

39a Match the questions and answers.

0	Do they often change their website?	[f]	**a**	Yes, I am.
1	Are Rob and Alex waiting for us?	☐	**b**	No, I don't.
2	Do you have breakfast every day?	☐	**c**	Yes, he is.
3	Are you working?	☐	**d**	No, he doesn't.
4	Does he live in London?	☐	**e**	Yes, they are.
5	Is Paul using the computer?	☐	**f**	No, they don't.

39b Choose and complete the sentences.

0 Hannah usually .... *eats* .... very healthy food, but she .... *'s eating* .... a big bar of chocolate at the moment. (eats, 's eating)

1 He .... in the studio now. He sometimes .... there in the mornings. (works, 's working)

2 I can't see very well because I .... my glasses. I .... them all the time. (don't wear, 'm not wearing)

3 No, I .... TV at the moment. I .... this programme every day. (don't watch, 'm not watching)

4 We often .... in the park, but we .... by the river now. (run, 're running)

5 They .... every match, of course, and they .... now. (don't win, aren't winning)

39c Circle the correct answer.

0 (Do you want)/Are you wanting a magazine?

1 Mark's in that shop. *He looks for /He's looking for* some trainers.

2 *Kate doesn't like /Kate isn't liking* oranges.

3 They're at the supermarket. *They get /They're getting* some milk and eggs.

4 What's this? What *do you read /are you reading*?

5 You're lying! *I don't believe /I'm not believing* you!

39d Complete the conversations. Use the present simple or present continuous of the verbs in brackets.

A: (0) ...*Does Natalie do*... (Natalie / do) any sport?

B: Yes – swimming and running. She's at the pool now. She (1) .... (have) a swimming lesson.

A: My dad isn't at work today, so he (2) .... (help) me with my computer project.

B: Lucky you! My dad (3) .... (not know) anything about computers, so he never (4) .... (help) me!

A: (5) .... (you / look) for this?

B: Oh yes! Thanks. I usually (6) .... (keep) it in my bag.

39e Complete the e-mail. Use the present simple or present continuous of the verbs in brackets.

⊖ ⊖ ⊖	New Message	▭

Hi, Sophie!

How are things? How are your mum and dad? I miss you all!
I (0) ....*like*........... (like) Brighton – it's very lively. We
(1) .... (not live) very near the sea, but our house is nice.

Mathew and Laura's new school is all right. They (2) ....
(get) a lot of homework and they (3) .... (have) a lot of tests – one every week. They (4) .... (hate) that!

Dad's new job is good. He's at home more. At the moment he
(5) .... (paint) the kitchen. Laura (6) ....
(make) a cake and Matthew (7) .... (play) in the garden.
It's nice and quiet here!

How are you? (8) .... (you / need) a holiday near the sea? Come and see us soon!

Love,
Bryony

Check 6 Present simple or present continuous

1 Complete the sentences. Use the present continuous of the verbs in brackets.

1 .... lunch?
(Mark / have)

2 David .... in the library. (work)

3 Lisa .... the computer. (not use)

4 Emma and Kate .... in the cafeteria. (sit)

5 .... to music?
(you / listen)

6 I .... something for my History project. (read)

/ 6

2 Complete the conversation. Use the present continuous of the verbs in the box.

do cook help not watch paint watch

A: What (7) .... you .... ?
Are you busy?

B: I (8) .... some spaghetti. I'm hungry. Do you want some?

A: No, thanks. Is Joe here?

B: Yes. He and Ben are in the sitting room.

A: (9) .... they .... a DVD?

B: Yes, they are. Sarah and Nina are there too, but they (10) .... it. Sarah (11) .... something for the school play.

A: (12) .... Nina .... her?

B: No, she isn't. Nina can't paint at all.

/ 6

3 Circle the correct answer.

13 A: Who *do you talk / are you talking* to?
B: Lucy. She's in town.

14 A: There are some cheap T-shirts here.
B: *I don't need / I'm not needing* any T-shirts at the moment.

15 A: Is that a nice café?
B: Yes. *We go / We're going* there every day.

16 A: *Do you understand / Are you understanding* question 6?
B: No.

17 A: Is Luke ready?
B: No, not yet. *He gets / He's getting* dressed.

18 A: Is this a good present for Jack?
B: No! *He hates / He's hating* jazz.

19 A: Why *are you laughing / do you laugh*?
B: Read this article in the paper!

20 A: Are they good friends?
B: Yes. *They do / They're doing* everything together.

/ 8

Total: / 20

✓ Self-check

Wrong answers	Look again at	Try CD-ROM
2, 4, 6, 8, 11	**Unit 37**	Exercise 37
1, 3, 5, 7, 9, 10, 12	**Unit 38**	Exercise 38
13, 14, 15, 16, 17, 18, 19, 20	**Unit 39**	Exercise 39

Now do **Check 6**

Past tenses

40   *I was late.*

I **was** late.   They **weren't** at the café yesterday.   **Were** you there?

●   We use the past simple of *be* to talk about the past.

●   We often use these time expressions with the past simple: *yesterday, last night/ week/month/year, two hours/days/weeks/months ago, in January, in 2004:*
    They weren' t at the café **yesterday**.   He wasn' t at home **last night**.

Affirmative	Negative	Question
I/he/she/it **was**	I/he/she/it **wasn't** (**was not**)	**Was** I/he/she/it?
you/we/they **were**	you/we/they **weren't** (**were not**)	**Were** you/we/they?

Short answers	Yes, I/he/she/it **was**.	Yes, you/we/they **were**.
	No, I/he/she/it **wasn't**.	No, you/we/they **weren't**.

▶▶   *For uses of be, see Unit 32.*

▶▶   *See Appendix 11: Short forms of verbs, page 171.*

P R A C T I C E

40a   **Circle the correct answer.**

    0   Helen (*was*)/*were* in hospital yesterday.

    1   These shoes *was* /*were* very expensive.

    2   That shop *was* /*were* shut last week.

    3   Joe *was* /*were* here last night.

    4   I *was* /*were* ill yesterday.

    5   We *was* /*were* very busy two weeks ago.

    6   Our hotel *was* /*were* very clean.

    7   You *was* /*were* brilliant!

    8   My parents *was* /*were* in Italy in March.

    9   I *was* /*were* very happy last year.

    10   Kate *was* /*were* at home yesterday.

40b **Complete the sentences. Use *was, wasn't, were* or *weren't*.**

   0 Last year I was at drama school. I ......*wasn't*...... at university.

   1 Jo was at drama school, too, but she .... at my school in Cardiff.

   2 Tim .... in Cardiff from January to April. He wasn't there in May.

   3 Justin and I were at the same school, but we .... in the same class.

   4 Mark and Amanda were in Cardiff last year, too, but they weren't at drama school. They .... at university.

   5 The course wasn't easy. Last term .... very difficult.

   6 I .... happy! I was worried a lot of the time.

40c **Write questions. Use *was* or *were*.**

   0 you / at home yesterday?   *Were you at home yesterday?*

   1 where / you? ....

   2 the museum / open? ....

   3 Sam / with you? ....

   4 why / he / late? ....

   5 you / annoyed? ....

   6 why / the tickets / expensive? ....

40d **Complete the short answers.**

   0 A: Was Nikki at college yesterday?   B: No, ...*she wasn't*...... .

   1 A: Was her driving test yesterday?   B: Yes, ...

   2 A: Was she worried about it?   B: No, ...

   3 A: Were you and Dan at college?   B: Yes, ...

   4 A: Were Jack and Luke there?   B: No, ...

   5 A: Was Jack ill?   B: Yes, ...

   6 A: Was Luke ill, too?   B: No, ...

40e **Complete the conversation. Use *was, wasn't, were* or *weren't*.**

A: I (0) ......*was*...... at the zoo yesterday with my sister and her little boy. We (1) .... there for his birthday.

B: Oh. (2) .... the zoo nice?

A: Yes, it (3) .... The elephants (4) .... amazing!

B: (5) .... they frightening?

A: No, they (6) .... They (7) .... just really big. What about you? Where (8) .... you yesterday morning?

B: I (9) .... at home. I (10) .... very busy.

41 *I walked to the station.*

I **walked** to the station.   They **stayed** at the café.   Sarah **arrived** at seven.

- We use the past simple to talk about actions and situations that started and finished in the past.
- To form the past simple of regular verbs, we add *-ed* to the verb. Be careful of the spelling changes:
  walk → walk**ed**   arrive → arrive**d**   stop → stop**ped**   try → tr**ied**

Affirmative I/you/he/she/it/we/they work**ed**

▶▶ *See Appendix 6: Spelling rules for verbs + -ed, page 170.*

▶▶ *For time words and expressions that we often use with the past simple, see Units 40 and 44.*

P R A C T I C E

41a **Complete the table.**

Infinitive	Past simple	Infinitive	Past simple
talk	*talked*	enjoy	
listen		marry	
carry		rain	
dance		live	
look		rob	
stop		want	
hope		plan	
ask		wash	

41b **Re-write the sentences. Use the past simple.**

0 We often play golf.   *We played golf* .... last week.

1 I cycle to college every day.   .... yesterday.

2 She watches television every night. .... last night.

3 They sometimes visit us.   .... in June.

4 I tidy my room every week.   .... last weekend.

5 He always phones me.   .... yesterday.

6 You work hard.   .... last month.

7 I always walk to work.   .... yesterday.

8 He usually stays with us.   .... last summer.

41c **Jodie was busy last year. Look at her notes and complete the sentences. Use the past simple.**

January: join drama group   May: play in orchestra

February: help with student magazine   June: organise end-of-year concert

March: design posters for play   July: visit Kelly in London

April: perform in play

0 In January she ....*joined*........ a drama group.

1 In February she .... with the student magazine.

2 In March she .... posters for a play.

3 In April she .... in a play.

4 In May she .... in the orchestra.

5 In June she .... a concert.

6 In July she .... her friend in London.

41d **Complete the newspaper article. Use the past simple of the verbs in brackets.**

In November, Patrick Woodhead, Tom Avery and Andrew Gerber (0) ....*started*........ (start) their journey to the South Pole. Forty six days later, they (1) .... (complete) it. They (2) .... (train) in London and New Zealand. In London, they (3) .... (pull) heavy car tyres around the parks, and in New Zealand they (4) .... (practise) climbing in snow. On the journey, they (5) .... (travel) on skis and (6) .... (try) to become the fastest British people to reach the South Pole. They (7) .... (succeed). But a week later, a woman, Fiona Thornewill, (8) .... (finish) the same journey in forty two days.

Now they are back in London and Woodhead is writing a book about the trip.

41e **Complete the extract from a story. Use the past simple of the verbs in the box.**

answer   ~~ask~~   decide   move   stay   study   want

'Where do you live?' he (0) ....*asked*........ . 'Here in Sheffield,'
I (1) .... 'I (2) .... History here, and after university
I (3) .... here. Now I'm a teacher. Do you live in Sheffield?' 'Yes. We
(4) .... here in August. We (5) .... to leave London and
we (6) .... to move north. We're very happy here. It's a great place.'

42 *We went to town.*

| We **went** to town yesterday. | I **bought** some magazines. | My sister **met** her friends. |

Some verbs do not form the past simple with *-ed*. They are irregular:
go → went   buy → bought   meet → met

Affirmative | I/you/he/she/it/we/they went

⚠ The past simple of *have got* is *had*: I **had** a terrible headache last night.

▶▶ **See Appendix 12: Irregular verbs, page 172.**

PRACTICE

42a Complete the table.

Infinitive	Past simple	Infinitive	Past simple
come	*came*	know	
put		understand	
get		do	
tell		speak	
cut		feel	
think		write	
let		sing	
bring		buy	
keep		fall	
win		forget	

42b Complete the sentences. Use the past simple of the verbs in the box.

| find   give   have   leave   meet   pay   go   ~~see~~   sit |

0   I .... *saw* .... Emma last night.

1   I .... dinner with her.

2   We .... at 7.30.

3   We .... a nice restaurant by the river.

4   We .... outside.

5   It was her birthday, so I .... her a CD.

6   I .... for our dinner.

7   We .... the restaurant at 10.30.

8   I .... to bed at 11.30.

42c **Write sentences. Use the past simple.**

0   Tim and I / go / to the beach yesterday   *Tim and I went to the beach yesterday.*

1   we / swim / in the sea   ....

2   Tim / take / some photos   ....

3   I / read / a magazine   ....

4   we / eat / our sandwiches   ....

5   I / run / along the beach   ....

6   we / have / a great time   ....

42d **Complete the extract from an e-mail. Use the past simple of the verbs in brackets.**

⬤ ⬤ ⬤   New Message   ▭

Last year I (0) ....*learnt*.......... (learn) how to ride a motorbike. I
(1) .... (buy) an old bike and then I (2) ....
(take) some lessons. My brother (3) .... (teach) me, too.

So, this summer, my brother and I (4) .... (go) to the
south of France on our bikes. We (5) .... (see) a lot of
different places and (6) .... (meet) some great people.
Every night we (7) .... (sleep) outside and in the morning
we (8) .... (wake up) with the sun. It was fantastic!

42e **Read the text and complete the sentences. Use the past simple.**

Jessica is working with some children this summer. Every day, she gets
up at 7.00, makes sandwiches for the children, drives them to the beach,
spends the day there, speaks to her mum on the phone and sends some
text messages to her friends. She usually feels tired in the evening. She
has dinner at 8.00 and goes to bed at 11.00.

Yesterday ...

0   She ....*got up*........ at 7.00.

1   She .... sandwiches for the children.

2   She .... the children to the beach.

3   She .... the day on the beach.

4   She .... to her mum on the phone in the evening.

5   She .... some text messages to her friends.

6   She .... tired in the evening.

7   She .... dinner at 8.00.

8   She .... to bed at 11.00.

43 I didn't see it. Did you see it?

I **didn't see** the film last night.	We **didn't like** the food.
Did you **see** the film last night?	**Did** you **like** the food?

Negative	I/you/he/she/it/we/they **didn't (did not) see**
Question	**Did** I/you/he/she/it/we/they **see**?
Short answers	Yes, I/you/he/she/it/we/they **did**.
	No, I/you/he/she/it/we/they **didn't**.

 We use *did/didn't* + infinitive in negative sentences and questions.
I didn't **see** the film last night. (Not ~~I didn't **saw** the film last night.~~)
Did you **like** the food? (Not ~~Did you **liked** the food?~~)

▶▶ **See Appendix 11: Short forms of verbs, page 171.**

P R A C T I C E

43a Complete the sentences. Use the negative form of the verbs.

0 Jessica went to the bookshop but she ....*didn't go*........ to the newsagent's.

1 Mark brought some orange juice but he .... any food.

2 We spoke to a lot of people but we .... to Tom.

3 They asked me about my experience but they .... me about my education.

4 You made a cup of coffee for her but you .... one for me!

5 I thought about him a lot but he .... about me.

6 The hotel had a pool but it .... a restaurant.

7 I read the first story but I .... the second one.

8 He sent a postcard to Beth but .... one to Kirsty.

43b Re-write the sentences. Use the past simple.

0 I don't often sleep well.   ....*I didn't sleep well*........ last night.

1 She doesn't write to me.   .... last week.

2 You don't often spend much.   .... yesterday.

3 He doesn't call me every day.   .... last night.

4 They don't often go on holiday.   .... in August.

5 We don't live in London.   .... last year.

6 Our team doesn't always win.   .... yesterday.

7 We don't watch TV every day.   .... yesterday.

8 I don't see her every day.   .... yesterday.

43c **Write questions. Use the past simple.**

    0 what / you / do / yesterday?   *What did you do yesterday?*
....

    1 you / go / anywhere?   ....

    2 Jack and Lucy / come / with you?   ....

    3 how / you / get / there?   ....

    4 where / you / meet / Nina?   ....

    5 you / have / a good time?   ....

43d **Complete the short answers.**

    0 **A:** Did Charlotte phone you yesterday?   **B:** Yes, *she did* ....

    1 **A:** Did you tell her about the accident?   **B:** Yes, ...

    2 **A:** Did she know about it?   **B:** No, ...

    3 **A:** Did the other car stop?   **B:** No, ...

    4 **A:** Did you and Joe call the police?   **B:** Yes, ...

    5 **A:** Did they ask you any questions?   **B:** Yes, ...

43e **Which of these things did you do last year? Write short answers that are true for you.**

    0 Did you leave school?   ....

    1 Did you start work?   ....

    2 Did you make any new friends?   ....

    3 Did you learn a new skill?   ....

    4 Did you go to a new place?   ....

    5 Did you change anything in your life?   ....

43f **Complete the conversation. Use the past simple of the verbs in brackets.**

A: When (0) .... *did you get* .... (you / get) here?

B: Last night.

A: What time (1) .... (you / leave) London?

B: At 7.30. We (2) .... (not stop) on the way, so it only took us four hours. (3) .... (you / come) by car?

A: No, I (4) .... I got the train.

B: (5) .... (somebody / meet) you at the station?

A: Yes. My friend met me in his car. But then we got lost on our way here. We (6) .... (not have) a map. In the end, we phoned the hotel and asked for directions!

B: You had a difficult journey!

44   *last night, two days ago*

> A: Did you phone her **last night**?   B: No, I phoned her **two days ago**.
> I met her **when I was in London**.

● We often use these time expressions with the past simple: *yesterday, last night/ week/weekend/month/year, two hours/days/weeks/months/years ago, in 2002/ April:*
  A: *Did you phone her* **last night**?   B: *No, I phoned her* **two days ago**.
● We can also use *when* + subject + verb in the past simple. Notice when we use a comma (,):
  I met her **when I was** *in London.*   **When I was five,** *we moved to Brighton.*

P R A C T I C E

44a **Complete the sentences. Use one word in each space.**

Today is Sunday 19th August.

  o   We had a party here last ....*night*........ . (8.00 p.m. – 11.00 p.m., 18th August)

  1   We were very busy last .... (12th – 18th August)

  2   We cleaned the house .... (18th August)

  3   I bought some new clothes three .... ago. (16th August)

  4   My cousin stayed with us .... weekend. (11th and 12th August)

  5   He left college three .... ago. (19th May)

  6   He moved here two weeks .... (5th August)

44b **Complete the extract from a magazine article. Use *when* and the past simple of the verbs in brackets.**

> I started writing (0) ....*when I was*................ (I / be) seven. I wrote lots of
> stories. (1) .... (we / come) to Britain, I stopped writing
> for a few years. I started writing again (2) .... (I / be)
> about fourteen. (3) .... (I / be) in my first year at
> university, I wrote a book about my family and our life in the Sudan before we came to
> Britain. We had a very different life (4) .... (we / live)
> there and I wanted to write about it. I was amazed (5) ....
> (the book / become) so popular!

Check 7 Past simple

1 Complete the sentences. Use the past simple of the verbs in brackets.

1 We .... at home on Saturday. (not be)

2 .... to Kate last night? (you / talk)

3 They .... the party at about 12.00. (leave)

4 We were late because we .... our bus. (miss)

5 .... with you last night? (Adam / be)

6 My brother .... this car two years ago. (buy)

7 Susan .... me with my Science project. (help)

8 We .... dinner with Rob and Anna on Saturday. (have)

/ 8

2 Complete the short answers.

9 A: Did you go anywhere yesterday?
B: Yes, ...

10 A: Was the film good?
B: Yes, ...

11 A: Did you get good seats?
B: No, ...

12 A: Were Kate and Nikki there?
B: No, ...

13 A: Was Kate at college in the afternoon?
B: No, ...

14 A: Did she stay at home?
B: Yes, ...

15 A: Did you call her?
B: Yes, ...

/ 7

3 Complete the sentences. Use the words in the box.

ago last when year yesterday

16 I had an exam ....

17 I got here two hours ....

18 We sold our car last ....

19 They were here .... week.

20 He moved to London .... he was twenty three.

/ 5

4 Complete the conversation. Use the past simple of the verbs in the box.

be enjoy love see try

A: So, (21) .... you .... your holiday?

B: Yes, thanks. Rome's a beautiful city! We (22) .... it. We (23) .... some lovely places. And the food was wonderful! We (24) .... lots of new things and they (25) .... all lovely.

/ 5

Total: / 25

45 *I was watching TV at six.*

> A: I **was watching** TV at six.   I **wasn't working**.   What **were** you **doing**?
> B: I **was talking** to Luke **while** Kate **was making** dinner.

We use the past continuous to talk about:

- an action that was in progress at a time in the past. The action started before that time and continued after that time: *I **was watching** TV at six.*

- two actions that were in progress at the same time in the past:
  *I **was talking** to Luke while Kate **was making** dinner.*

  We use *while* with the two verbs. Notice when we use a comma (,):
  *I was talking to Luke **while** Kate was making dinner.*
  ***While** Kate was making dinner, I was talking to Luke.*

Affirmative	I/he/she/it **was watching**	you/we/they **were watching**
Negative	I/he/she/it **wasn't** (**was not**) **watching**	you/we/they **weren't** (**were not**) **watching**
Question	**Was** I/he/she/it **watching**?	**Were** you/we/they **watching**?
Short answers	Yes, I/he/she/it **was**.	Yes, you/we/they **were**.
	No, I/he/she/it **wasn't**.	No, you/we/they **weren't**.

▶▶ ***See Appendix 5: Spelling rules for verbs + -ing, page 170.***

PRACTICE

45a **Complete the sentences. Use the past continuous of the verbs in brackets.**

At half past five yesterday afternoon...

0 Sam and I ....*were waiting*.... at the bus stop. (wait)

1 It .... (rain)

2 We were cold and wet because we .... coats or jackets. (not wear)

3 Some people behind us .... (talk)

4 Sam .... to them. (not listen)

5 He .... me about his football match. (tell)

6 A young woman .... at the side of the road. (stand)

7 She .... a big sports bag. (carry)

8 She .... but she looked very unhappy. (not cry)

45b **Write questions. Use the past continuous.**

0 what / the two men / wear?   *What were the two men wearing?*

1 why / you / laugh?   ....

2 it / snow?   ....

3 Sarah / show / you her photos?   ....

4 where / they / go?   ....

5 Tom / have / lunch?   ....

6 Amy / wear / her new shoes?   ....

45c **Complete the short answers.**

0 **A:** Were you watching TV at seven?   **B:** No, *I wasn't* .

1 **A:** Were you making dinner?   **B:** Yes, ...

2 **A:** Was Hannah tidying her room?   **B:** No, ...

3 **A:** Was she doing her homework?   **B:** Yes, ...

4 **A:** Were Ella and Adam doing theirs?   **B:** No, ...

5 **A:** Was Mark working?   **B:** Yes, ...

45d **Complete the sentences. Use *while* and the past continuous of the verbs in the box.**

| clean   climb   do   ~~drive~~   ~~lie~~   not watch   play   read   shine   talk |

0 Kim .... *was lying* .... on the beach ....*while*.... Ben ......*was driving*........
to the airport.

1 .... you .... football, I .... a book.

2 The sun .... we .... the mountain.

3 I .... television .... I .... to you.

4 .... Jamie .... the shopping, Laura and Becky
.... the kitchen.

45e **Complete the conversations. Use the past continuous of the verbs in brackets.**

A: (0) .... *Were you working* .... (you / work) in the studio at eleven?

B: No. I was at a lecture. And while Mr Allan (1) .... (talk)
about Picasso, I (2) .... (think) about my trip to Spain!

A: What (3) .... (you / do) at eight o'clock last night?

B: We (4) .... (get) ready for the party today. I
(5) .... (cook) while Lisa (6) .... (move)
the furniture out of the sitting room.

46 *I was going home when you rang.*

I **was going** home when you **rang**.   When he **arrived**, we **were having** dinner.

- We can use the past simple and past continuous together to talk about an action that happened while another action was in progress. We use the past continuous for the longer action that was in progress. We use the past simple for the shorter, finished action: *I **was going** home when you **rang**.*

- We use *when* before the action in the past simple. Notice when we use a comma (,):
  *I was going home **when** you rang.   **When** you rang, I was going home.*

 Compare:
  *I **was going** home when you rang.* (I started going home before you rang.)
  *I **went** home when you rang.* (I started going home after, or at the time you rang.)

PRACTICE

46a Complete the sentences. Use the past simple or past continuous of the verbs in brackets.

o When I heard the news about Alex, I ....*was watching*........ TV. (watch)

1 We .... to work when we saw the accident. (drive)

2 Jessica was doing her homework when the fire .... (start)

3 She was sleeping when somebody .... her computer. (steal)

4 When the lift stopped, we .... up to the fourth floor. (go)

5 When we saw him, he .... by his car. (stand)

6 We were walking on the beach when we .... David. (see)

46b Circle the correct answer.

o We *sat /* *were sitting* in the park when it *started / was starting* to rain.

1 When I *met / was meeting* him, he *studied / was studying* Biology.

2 She *worked / was working* when I *phoned / was phoning* her.

3 *Did you go / Were you going* to college when I *saw / was seeing* you, or were you on your way to the sports centre?

4 When I *saw / was seeing* Paul, he *didn't watch / wasn't watching* TV. He was in the kitchen.

5 *Did Lucy have / Was Lucy having* breakfast when you *left / were leaving* the house, or was she in bed?

6 We *drove / were driving* home when the police *stopped / were stopping* us.

46c **Complete what Anna says about herself. Use the past simple or past continuous of the verbs in brackets.**

I (0) ....**went**............ (go) to university when I left school. I
(1) .... (study) Geography there when I (2) ....
(hear) about the Erasmus programme for European students. I decided to go to
a university in Germany as part of this programme. I learnt a lot at the university
and I went on some interesting student trips.

When the course finished, I (3) .... (not come) home immediately.
I travelled around the country for a month. I (4) .... (stay) in a
hostel in Heidelberg when I (5) .... (meet) some nice students.
When I left, I (6) .... (give) them my address, and they're
coming to visit me next year, so I can practise my German again then!

46d **Complete the conversations. Use the past simple or past continuous of the verbs in the box.**

arrive   cycle   fall   go (x2)   hear   ~~listen~~
meet   see (x2)   stop   take   wait

A: I (0) ....**was listening**............ to the radio last night when I (1) ....
something about that new shop in West Street.

B: Really? What?

A: Where (2) .... you .... when I (3) .... you in
town this morning?

B: To the station. I didn't talk to you because I was late for my train. Sorry!

A: How did you break your arm?

B: I broke it last week. I (4) .... down a hill when I
(5) .... off my bike.

A: How did you get to hospital?

B: A driver (6) .... when he (7) .... me in the
road. He (8) .... me to the hospital.

A: Did you have a nice afternoon?

B: Yes, thanks. We went to Brighton. And when we (9) .... Laura
and Paul, we (10) .... for a walk in the park. It was lovely.

A: (11) .... Mark .... for you when you (12) .... at
the airport?

B: Yes. Phil was with him, too.

Check 8 Past continuous and past simple

1 Complete the conversation. Use the past simple or past continuous of the verbs in brackets.

A: (1) .... (you / be) by the river at four o'clock?

B: Yes. We (2) .... (sit) under some trees, near the bridge. A lot of people (3) .... (swim) in the river.

A: (4) .... (Adam / be) with you?

B: Adam? No, he was at home. He (5) .... (work) on his History project.

A: What about Tim and Sarah? (6) .... (they / be) at home, too?

B: Yes. They (7) .... (revise) for their exams.

| / 7 |

2 Circle the correct answer.

8 We started dancing when Jack *played / was playing* some good music.

9 When I saw Kate, I *told / was telling* her about the accident.

10 Were you on the train or *did you walk / were you walking* home when I sent you my text message?

11 I shouted 'Jo!' when I *saw / was seeing* her on the other side of the street.

12 My brother *played / was playing* tennis when he hurt his leg.

13 Who was he talking to when we *arrived / were arriving*?

14 She *waited / was waiting* for the bus when I saw her.

| / 7 |

3 Complete the conversation. Use one word in each gap.

A: What were you doing this afternoon (15) .... I phoned?

B: I (16) .... lying on the sofa (17) .... my sister was telling me about her friend's party and Becky and Lisa (18) .... reading magazines. (19) .... you and Kirsty in town?

| / 5 |

4 Complete the extract from a story. Use the past simple or past continuous of the verbs in brackets.

Lucy became a model in an unusual way. Last year, she (20) .... (wait) for a bus when a woman (21) .... (ask) her: 'Would you like to be a model?' She (22) .... (give) Lucy her business card and Lucy (23) .... (join) her agency about a month later.

I (24) .... (see) Lucy last June. She was working in London while I (25) .... (do) my exams at university.

| / 6 |

| Total: / 25 |

Perfect tenses

47 I've forgotten his name.

| I've forgotten his name. | She hasn't washed the car. | Have you made a cake? |

We use the present perfect to talk about an action that happened in the past and has a result in the present:

I've forgotten his name. (I can't remember it now.)
She hasn't washed the car. (It isn't clean now.)

Affirmative	Negative	Question
I/you/we/they**'ve** (have) forgotten	I/you/we/they **haven't** (have not) forgotten	**Have** I/you/we/they forgotten?
he/she/it**'s** (has) forgotten	he/she/it **hasn't** (has not) forgotten	**Has** he/she/it forgotten?

Short answers	Yes, I/you/we/they **have.**	No, I/you/we/they **haven't.**
	Yes, he/she/it **has.**	No, he/she/it **hasn't.**

To form the present perfect, we use *have/has* + the past participle of the verb. To form the past past participle of regular verbs, we add *-ed* to the verb:

clean → *clean**ed**   work → work**ed***

▶▶ **For the past participles of regular verbs, see Appendix 6: Spelling rules for verbs + -ed, page 170. For the past participles of irregular verbs, see Appendix 12: Irregular verbs, page 172.**

P R A C T I C E

47a Complete the sentences. Use the present perfect of the verbs in brackets.

0 These cups are clean. Laura ....**'s washed**........ them. (wash)

1 The table's next to the sofa now. We .... it. (move)

2 You can use your bike now. I .... it. (mend)

3 Ryan looks different. He .... a lot of weight. (lose)

4 She can't walk. She .... her leg. (break)

5 The boys aren't here. They .... their friends to the airport. (take)

6 It .... raining. We can leave now. (stop)

7 I can't open the door. Jack .... it. (lock)

8 Let's take some photos. I .... my camera. (bring)

47b **Complete the conversations. Use the present perfect of the verbs in the box.**

| not come | not invite | ~~not open~~ | not pack | not read | not see | not turn |

o **A:** What's in that box? **B:** I don't know. I ...... *haven't opened* ...... it.

1 **A:** Are Joe and Nicole here? **B:** No. They .... home.

2 **A:** Is he going to her party? **B:** No. She .... him.

3 **A:** Where are my keys? **B:** I don't know. I .... them.

4 **A:** Is Luke ready? **B:** No. He .... his bag.

5 **A:** Is the television on? **B:** Yes. We .... it off.

6 **A:** Is that a good book? **B:** I don't know. I .... it.

47c **Write questions. Then complete the short answers. Use the present perfect.**

o Emma and Sam / wake up?
A: *Have Emma and Sam woken up?* ...... **B:** Yes, *they have* ....

1 they / have / breakfast?
A: .... **B:** No, ...

2 Emma / get / dressed?
A: .... **B:** No, ...

3 Sam / make / any coffee?
A: .... **B:** Yes, ...

4 he / walk / the dog?
A: .... **B:** No, ...

5 you / finish / your breakfast?
A: .... **B:** Yes, ...

6 you / have / a shower?
A: .... **B:** No, ...

47d **Complete the conversation. Use the present perfect of the verbs in brackets.**

A: Can you help me? This girl (o) ...... *'s fallen* ...... (fall) off her bike. She
(1) .... (hurt) her leg.

B: My leg's OK, I think. But this arm really hurts. (2) ....
(I / break) it?

C: I don't know, but don't worry. (3) .... (you / hurt) your head?

B: No, I (4) ....

C: Good. I'll call an ambulance. Can we call somebody for you? A relative?

B: I'm staying with a friend. Her number's in my address book but I
(5) .... (not / bring) that with me. Is my bike all right?

A: I don't know. I (6) .... (not / look) at it. Don't worry about
your bike. Just relax.

48 *I've already told her.*

> I**'ve already told** her. I **haven't asked** Sam **yet**.
> **Have** you **asked** Sarah **yet**? I**'ve just spoken** to her.

- We often use *already*, *yet* and *just* with the present perfect.
- *Already* means 'before now': *I've **already** told her.*
- *Yet* means 'up to now'. We use it in negative sentences and questions:
  *I haven't asked Sam **yet**.* *Have you asked Sarah **yet**?*
- *Just* means 'a very short time ago': *I've **just** spoken to her.*

 Already and *just* come after *have/has*. *Yet* comes at the end of the statement or question.

PRACTICE

48a Complete the conversations. Use *already* and the present perfect of the verbs in brackets.

o	A: Don't forget to call Tom.	B: I *'ve already called* him. (call)
1	A: Shall I wash the car?	B: Jack .... it. (wash)
2	A: I'll ask Sarah about this.	B: We .... her. (ask)
3	A: When are they leaving?	B: They .... (leave)
4	A: Can I borrow your skirt?	B: I .... it to Jo. (lend)
5	A: Coffee?	B: No. I .... some. (have)
6	A: This is Adam, my cousin.	B: I know. We .... (meet)
7	A: Do you need a ticket?	B: No. I .... one. (buy)
8	A: We must lock the door.	B: Mum .... it. (lock)

48b Look at Leah's list of things to do and write sentences. Use *already* or *not ... yet* and the present perfect.

clean room
buy some aspirin ✓
phone Nicole ✓
write to Kate
finish project
pick up jacket from cleaner's ✓
iron skirt
wash T-shirts ✓

o ... *She hasn't cleaned her room yet.*
oo ... *She's already bought some aspirin.*
1 ....
2 ....
3 ....
4 ....
5 ....
6 ....

48c **Write questions. Use the present perfect with *yet*.**

0	you / buy / the tickets?	*Have you bought the tickets yet?*
1	you / plan / the journey?	....
2	Sam and Joe / book / the hotel?	....
3	Sam / tell / his parents?	....
4	you / learn / any Spanish?	....
5	Joe / pack / his bag?	....
6	you / find / your passport?	....

48d **Complete the conversation. Use *just* and the present perfect of the verbs in brackets.**

Jess: Mum, Lucy (0) ....*'s just phoned*........ (phone). She wants to come round. Is that OK?

Mum: Can she come later? We (1) .... (get) home – and we haven't had dinner yet.

Jess: Hi, Lucy. We're a bit busy at the moment. My parents (2) .... (come) home. Can you come later? And – I (3) .... (remember) – could I borrow your tent this weekend? Kirsty (4) .... (ask) me to go camping with her.

Lucy: Oh, sorry! I (5) .... (arrange) a camping trip with Melissa, so I'll need my tent.

Jess: Never mind. I'll ask someone else.

Mum: Jessica!

Jess: I've got to go, Lucy. Mum (6) .... (call) me. See you later!

48e **Circle the correct answer.**

A: Have you read that book (0) *just /*(yet)?

B: No. Do you want to read it?

A: No, thanks. I've (1) *already /yet* read it.

A: Has Ben sold his car (2) *just /yet*?

B: No. He hasn't advertised it (3) *already /yet*. Why? Are you interested in it?

A: Yes. My sister's looking for a car. She's (4) *just /yet* got a new job and she needs a car for it.

A: Have you looked at your form (5) *just /yet*?

B: Yes. I've (6) *already /yet* sent it back.

A: Do you like my room? I've (7) *just /yet* painted it.

B: Yes, it's great. Are you getting some new furniture, too?

A: Yes, but it hasn't come (8) *already /yet*.

49 *I've never been to India.*

> I**'ve never been** to India. I**'ve worked** in a hotel.
> **Have** you **ever seen** any Indian films? This is the first time we**'ve come** by train.

- We can use the present perfect to talk about experiences in our lives up to now:
  I've never *been* to India. *I've worked* in a hotel.

- We often use *never* and *ever* when we talk about experiences in our lives. We use *never* in statements and *ever* in questions:
  I've **never** been to India. *Have you* **ever** seen any Indian films?

- We often use *This is/It's the first time* with the present perfect to talk about something that is happening for the first time:
  This is/It's the first time we've come by train.

 Note the difference between *been* (*to*) and *gone* (*to*):
  He**'s been** to India. (He went to India but he is back now.)
  He**'s gone** to India. (He is in India now.)

PRACTICE

49a Tim wants to get a part in a film. Look at the table and complete the sentences. Use the present perfect.

	had a part in a film	been on TV	ridden a horse	driven a car	played the piano	sung jazz songs
Rob	✗	✓	✗	✓	✗	✓
Kaya	✓	✓	✗	✓	✓	✗
Tim	✗	✗	✓	✗	✓	✓

0 Rob ....*'s never had*........ a part in a film, but he ....*'s been*........
   on TV.

1 Kaya .... the piano, but she .... jazz
   songs.

2 Rob and Kaya .... a horse but they ....
   a car.

3 I .... a horse and I .... the piano.

4 The film company wants an actor who can ride a horse, play the
   piano and sing jazz songs. I've done all those things, but I
   .... a part in a film. I don't think I'll get this part.

85

49b **Write questions. Use the present perfect with *ever*.**

0   you / use / this machine?   *Have you ever used this machine?*

1   you / be / late for a meeting?   ....

2   the director / speak / to you?   ....

3   you / visit / this website?   ....

4   Kim and Zoe / have / lunch with you? ....

5   you / be / to that café?   ....

6   Tom / phone / you?   ....

49c **Circle the correct answer.**

0   Let's ask Sam about Hong Kong. He's (been)/*gone* there.

1   Jason isn't here. He's *been* /*gone* to the sports centre.

2   Is this your medicine? Have you *been* /*gone* to the doctor today?

3   We've *been* /*gone* to the shop and we've got some juice. Do you want some?

4   They've *been* /*gone* to the cinema. Do you want to leave a message for them?

5   I've *been* /*gone* to that exhibition. It's really good.

6   Emma's not in the library. Has she *been* /*gone* home?

7   The boys have *been* /*gone* to the park. They'll be back at six.

8   Nikki's *been* /*gone* to Spain lots of times.

49d **Complete the conversation. Use the present perfect of the verbs in brackets.**

A: Can you read the map? This is the first time I (0) ....*'ve driven*........... (drive) in London.

B: Yes, sure. Don't worry. Let's listen to a CD. Do you know this one by José Gonzalez?

A: No. I (1) .... (never / hear) anything by him.

B: I think he's good. He's coming to the Latitude Festival next month.
(2) .... (you / ever / be) to that?

A: No, I haven't. Is it good?

B: Paul thinks it's good. He (3) .... (be) to it. Oh! What was that? What's happened?

A: Oh no! We've got a flat tyre! This is the first time this (4) ....
(happen) to me! I don't know how to change it. My dad (5) ....
(never / show) me how to do it.

B: Can he come and help us?

A: No, my parents aren't at home this weekend. They (6) ....
(go) to Nottingham!

50 *I've known Jack for six months.*

> I**'ve known** Jack **for** six months.   He**'s been** a student here **since** September.
> **How long have** you **known** him?

- We can use the present perfect to talk about something that started in the past and continues in the present:
  I**'ve known** *Jack for six months.* (I met him six months ago and I know him now.)
- We often use *for* and *since* with the present perfect.
  - We use *for* to say how long something has continued:
    I've been here **for** *a week.* (I came here a week ago and I am here now.)
  - We use *since* to say when something began:
    He's been a student here **since** *September.* (He became a student in September and he is a student now.)
- We often use *how long* in questions: *How long have you known him?*

PRACTICE

50a **Complete the table. Write the words and phrases in the box in the correct group.**

> a few minutes   a long time   centuries   eight months   half past five
> last week   March   midnight   ten days   this morning   three weeks
> Tuesday   twelve years   two hours   yesterday   2004

for		since	
a few minutes			

50b **Complete the sentences. Use the present perfect of the verbs in brackets and *for* or *since*.**

0   My parents ....*have been*.... married ....*for*.... twenty five years. (be)

1   She .... here .... 2001. (live)

2   We .... our car .... a few months. (have)

3   I .... ill .... Sunday. (be)

4   She .... a cold .... four days. (have)

5   Emma's my best friend. I .... her .... five years. (know)

6   My brother .... football .... the World Cup in 1998. (love)

7   Kate and Mark .... in town .... nine o'clock. (be)

8   She .... here .... three months. (work)

50c Write questions. Use the present perfect with *how long*.

0 you / be / at this college? *How long have you been at this college?*

1 you / have / your car? ....

2 you / live / in the country? ....

3 this college / be / open? ....

4 it / have / these sports facilities? ....

5 you / know / Adam and Scott? ....

6 they / be / in the football team? ....

7 your brother / work / here? ....

8 you / have / your dog? ....

50d Complete the conversation. Use one word in each space.

Nina: Hi. Sorry we're late! (0) ....*How*........ long have you been here?

Matt: Not long. I've been here (1) .... five minutes, and Jack's been here (2) .... half past eight.

Nina: This is my friend, Becky.

Jack: Hi, Becky. Are you at college with Nina?

Becky: No, I've just started working at the hospital.

Jack: Really? My sister's a nurse there.

Becky: How (3) .... has she been there?

Jack: I think she's been there (4) .... last summer. Do you like working at the hospital?

Becky: Yes, I do. I've wanted to work with sick people (5) .... a long time. What do you do, Matt?

Matt: I'm a student, like Nina. We're on the same course. And Jack works for his dad.

Jack: Yes. My dad's owned a company (6) .... 2003. We make cakes.

Becky: Mm! I'd like that job! Do you eat them yourself?

Jack: Sometimes!

CineLand

50e Complete the sentences so they are true for you. Use *for* or *since*.

0 I've lived *in London for sixteen years* .

1 I've had ....

2 I've known ....

3 I've wanted ....

4 I've been ....

5 I've loved ....

51 *He's gone to town. / He went to town yesterday.*

> Rob**'s gone** to town. He'll be back this evening.   Sam **went** to town yesterday.

Present perfect

We use the present perfect to talk about something that happened or started in the past and has a connection with the present. We do not say when the action happened.

PAST   **PRESENT**

*Rob's **gone** to town.*
*We**'ve lived** here for ten years.*

Past simple

We use the past simple to talk about something that started and finished in the past. There is no connection with the present. Sometimes we say or ask when the action happened.

PAST   **PRESENT**

*Sam **went** to town yesterday.*
*We **lived** in London a year ago.*

PRACTICE

51a **Choose and complete the sentences.**

0 (He's been, He was)

Jack's very ill. ....*He's been*.......... in hospital for a week.

..........*He was*.......... ill last week, but he's OK now.

1 (Have you seen, Did you see)

.... my keys? I can't find them.

.... Mark last night?

2 (I've read, I read)

.... a great book about Italy last year.

.... a lot about climate change and I'm very worried about it.

3 (We haven't finished, We didn't finish)

.... our project. Can we give it to you tomorrow?

.... our conversation last night. Let's talk again this evening.

4 (They've gone, They went)

.... to Nicole's party last night.

Matthew and Anna aren't here. .... to the supermarket.

5 (He's broken, He broke)

.... his arm two weeks ago.

Grandad can't read the newspaper. .... his glasses.

6 (They've moved, They moved)

They don't live here. .... to Cambridge.

.... to London three months ago.

51b Complete the conversations. Use the present perfect or past simple of the verbs in brackets.

A: (o) ......*Have you ever been*...... (you / ever / be) to Spain?

B: Yes. We (1) .... (go) to Madrid last year.

A: Is your brother in Thailand now?

B: Yes. He (2) .... (phone) last night. He's fine.

A: I (3) .... (see) Jason last night.

B: Really? How is he?

A: Fine. He (4) .... (just / come) back from Australia.

A: Where's Becky? She (5) .... (be) here ten minutes ago.

B: She (6) .... (go) to town.

A: Would you like a biscuit? I (7) .... (make) some.

B: Oh, lovely! Yes, please. When (8) .... (you / make) them?

A: This morning. I hope they're OK.

51c Circle the correct answer.

A: (o) (*I've lost*)/ *I lost* my phone. I can't find it anywhere.

B: (1) *I've seen* / *I saw* it on the sofa yesterday.

A: (2) *Mum's tidied* / *Mum tidied* the sitting room, so there's nothing on the sofa now.

B: Here it is! (3) *She's put* / *She put* it on top of the bookcase.

A: Great! Thanks. I want to call Ryan. (4) *He's left* / *He left* a message last night. We're having lunch together today. We're going to the Hard Rock Café. (5) *Have you been* / *Were you* there?

B: Yes. (6) *I've had* / *I had* a meal there last week. It's nice.

51d Complete the magazine article. Use the present perfect or past simple of the verbs in brackets.

Gemma's a dancer. She performs in videos for pop groups. She (0) ......*'s been*...... (be) a dancer for seven years. She (1) .... (have) her first dance lesson when she was five. When she was eighteen, she (2) .... (move) to London and she (3) .... (join) a dance agency. 'I really love my job,' she says. 'I (4) .... (work) with some famous stars and I (5) .... (learn) a lot. I'm going to move to the United States because there are a lot of opportunities there. I (6) .... (be) there three times and I really like it. Last time I (7) .... (go) to some great classes and I (8) .... (meet) some interesting people. I'd really like to dance for somebody like Beyoncé.'

Check 9 Present perfect

1 Put the words in the correct order.

1 just / has / left / she

....

2 yet / have / told / they / her?

....

3 already / lunch / had / we / have

....

4 you / to / ever / Ireland / been / have?

....

5 not / he / phoned / yet / has

....

6 tried / never / Indian food / have / I

....

7 Matt / ever / a horse / ridden / has?

....

/ 7

2 Circle the correct answer.

8 They aren't here. They've *been / gone* to the cinema.

9 She's been an actress *for / since* 1997.

10 I've *never / ever* played basketball.

11 Nikki's *yet / just* called. She can't come with us.

12 We haven't seen Sarah *for / since* years.

13 Lucy's worked here *for / since* May.

14 We love Madrid. We've *been / gone* there lots of times.

15 Steven's had his car *for / since* seven months.

/ 8

3 Complete the conversation. Use the present perfect of the verbs in brackets.

A: (16) .... (you / move)?

B: Yes, we (17) .... Our new flat's really nice. And my room's lovely. Laura (18) .... (give) me some really nice posters and I (19) .... (order) a new bookcase but it (20) .... (not come) yet.

/ 5

4 Complete the extract from a letter. Use the present perfect or past simple of the verbs in brackets.

I'm having a great time in London.
I (21) .... (be) here since Monday and I (22) .... (meet) a lot of nice people. I'm staying at my sister's flat. She (23) .... (live) in London for two years and knows a lot of people here.
She (24) .... (have) a party on Saturday and a lot of her friends (25) .... (come) to it.

/ 5

Total: / 25

✓ Self-check

Wrong answers	Look again at	Try CD-ROM
16, 17, 18, 19	**Unit 47**	Exercise 47
1, 2, 3, 5, 11, 20	**Unit 48**	Exercise 48
4, 6, 7, 8, 10, 14	**Unit 49**	Exercise 49
9, 12, 13, 15	**Unit 50**	Exercise 50
21, 22, 23, 24, 25	**Unit 51**	Exercise 51

Now do **Check 9**

Future forms

52 *I'm going to stay at home.*

> A: **I'm going to stay** at home tomorrow. **Are** you **going to watch** the match tonight?
> B: No, we **aren't going to be** at home.

- We use *be going to* + infinitive to talk about things we have decided to do or not to do in the future: *I'm **going to stay** at home tomorrow.*
- We often use these time expressions when we talk about the future:
  *tonight, tomorrow, next week/month/year, in January, in the summer, on Monday, this week/weekend/month: Are you going to watch the match **tonight**?*

Affirmative	I'm (am) going to stay	he/she/it's (is) going to stay	you/we/they're (are) going to stay
Negative	I'm not (am not) going to stay	he/she/it isn't (is not) going to stay	you/we/they aren't (are not) going to stay
Question	Am I going to stay?	Is he/she/it going to stay?	Are you/we/they going to stay?
Short answers	Yes, I am.	Yes, he/she/it is.	Yes, you/we/they are.
	No, I'm not.	No, he/she/it isn't.	No, you/we/they aren't.

P R A C T I C E

52a **Complete Matt's plans for the weekend. Use *be going to* and the verbs in the box.**

ask	come	have	help	see	~~stay~~	take	use	visit

0 I .....*'m going to stay*..... in bed on Saturday morning.

1 In the afternoon, I .... my grandparents.

2 I .... a film with my cousins on Saturday night.

3 We .... a pizza in town before the film.

4 My friend Emma .... with us.

5 On Sunday morning, my parents .... us to the beach.

6 On Sunday afternoon, Emma .... me with my Business Studies project.

7 We .... my brother's laptop.

8 I .... him about it tonight!

52b **Complete the sentences. Use *be going to* and the verbs in brackets.**

0 I'm going to buy some clothes, but I .....*'m not going to spend*..... a lot of money. (not spend)

1 Tom's going to stay in bed on Sunday morning. He .... early. (not get up)

2 Lucy's going to meet Charlotte tomorrow, but they .... lunch together. (not have)

3 We're going to stay in a hotel. We .... with our cousins. (not stay)

4 Jo's going to take her skirt back to the shop. She ....it. (not keep)

5 I'm going to work with animals. I .... in an office. (not work)

6 My parents are going to paint the kitchen, but they .... my bedroom. (not paint)

52c **Write questions. Use *be going to*.**

0 you / phone / her tonight?   *Are you going to phone her tonight?*

1 she / stay / with you on Sunday?   ....

2 your friends / have / a party?   ....

3 we / tell / Ryan about Becky?   ....

4 what / you / do / in the summer?   ....

5 Matt / learn / to drive next year?   ....

6 where / they / stay?   ....

7 you / see / Justin tomorrow?   ....

8 he / move / here in September?   ....

52d **Complete the conversation. Use *be going to* and the verbs in brackets.**

A: Coralie and Thomas (0) .....*are going to visit*..... (visit) us next weekend. Do you remember them?

B: Yes, I do. What about Pauline? (1) .... (she / come), too?

A: No, she (2) .... She wants to come in October.

B: What (3) .... (you / do) with them?

A: We (4) .... (take) them to London on Saturday. We (5) .... (not stay) in a hotel. We (6) .... (go) for the day. Would you like to come with us?

B: Oh, yes. Thank you.

53 *I'll come with you.*

I'll come with you.	We won't be late.	Will the library be open tomorrow?

- We use *will* + infinitive without *to* to talk about something that we think, believe or know will happen in the future: *We won't be late.*
- We can also use *will* when we suddenly decide to do something:
  A: I'm leaving.   *B: I'll come with you.*

Affirmative	I/you/he/she/it/we/they'll (will) come
Negative	I/you/he/she/it/we/they won't (will not) come
Question	Will I/you/he/she/it/we/they come?
Short answers	Yes, I/you/he/she/it/we/they will.
	No, I/you/he/she/it/we/they won't.

▶▶   ***See Appendix 11: Short forms of verbs, page 171.***

P R A C T I C E

53a Complete the sentences. Use *will* and the verbs in brackets.

    0   The shops ....*will be*............... very busy tomorrow. Let's go on Monday. (be)

    1   I'm nervous about the party. I .... anybody. (not know)

    2   Kirsty .... those earrings. They're beautiful. (love)

    3   We .... this match without Tom. He's our best player. (not win)

    4   That train's always very crowded. You .... a seat. (not get)

    5   Ask Lisa. She .... you some money. (lend)

    6   Rome's a beautiful city. You .... a great time. (have)

53b Complete the conversations. Use *will*.

    0   **A:** Ben will be twenty next month.
        B: No, he .....*won't*..... . ...*He'll be*............... twenty in March.

    1   **A:** I won't remember anything in the exam.
        B: Yes, you .... everything.

    2   **A:** You'll need your sunglasses.
        B: No, I .... my umbrella.

    3   **A:** Beth won't bring any food.
        B: Yes, she .... some salad.

    4   **A:** We'll see her again tomorrow.
        B: No, we .... her on Friday.

    5   **A:** I won't have enough money for a bike.
        B: Yes, you .... £200.

53c **Complete the conversation. Use *I'll* or *I won't* and the verbs in the box.**

| get | ~~leave~~ | not eat | not get | not have | talk | wait |

Jason: Hi, Sam. Are you ready for a break?

Sam: Yes. (0) ....*I'll leave*............... my books here.

Jason: Do you want a sandwich?

Sam: Um ... no. (1) .... anything now, thanks.

Jason: Do you want to talk to Jessica?

Sam: No, it's OK. (2) .... to her later. (3) .... a long break – just ten minutes. My exam's tomorrow.

Jason: Yes, mine is, too. Do you want to get the seven o'clock bus tomorrow?

Sam: Um ... no, (4) .... that one. (5) .... the next one.

Jason: Fine. Wait a minute. I need to get my bottle of water.

Sam: OK. (6) .... for you here.

Jason: OK. See you in a minute.

54 *I'm going to stay. / I'll stay.*

We use *be going* to for things we have decided to do. We use *will* when we suddenly decide to do something. Compare:

A: *What are your plans for next Saturday?*   B: *I**'m going to stay** at home.*

A: *There's Jo. I need to talk to her for a minute.*   B: *OK. I**'ll stay** here.*

PRACTICE

54a **Circle the correct answer.**

0 Next week (*I'm going to visit*)/*I'll visit* my sister in Rome.

1 Oh no! I forgot to call Mark last night. *I'm going to call /I'll call* him now.

2 *I'm going to have /I'll have* some guitar lessons next term.

3 I can't remember their address. Oh, wait a minute – *I'm going to look /I'll look* in my address book.

4 Look. Jane's here. *I'm going to go /I'll go* and talk to her.

5 *I'm going to do /I'll do* a short computer course in January.

6 *I'm going to buy /I'll buy* a car next year.

7 Look. These T-shirts are fantastic! *I'm going to get /I'll get* two.

8 *I'm going to wear /I'll wear* my new jeans to Becky's party on Saturday.

54b **Complete the conversations. Use *will* or *be going to* and the verbs in brackets.**

0 **A:** Are you ready to leave now?

B: Yes. I ....*'ll get*........... my coat. (get)

1 **A:** Is your birthday on the twenty fifth?

B: Yes, and I .... a party. Here's your invitation! (have)

2 **A:** Would you like to join the drama group?

B: That's a good idea! I .... about it. (think)

3 **A:** This coat's nice.

B: Which one? Oh yes, it's lovely. I .... back tomorrow and look at it. I haven't got time now. (come)

4 **A:** Have you got a mobile?

B: No, but I .... one next month. (get)

5 **A:** Can I talk to you or are you busy?

B: No, it's OK. I .... that later. (read)

6 **A:** Why are you putting those books in boxes?

B: I .... them. I don't want them. (sell)

7 **A:** I .... Sam and Jessica on Saturday. Would you like to come with me? (visit)

B: Yes, I'd love to.

8 **A:** What's the largest city in the USA?

B: Hmm ... I don't know. Wait. I .... my dad. (ask)

54c **Complete the conversation. Use *will* or *be going to* and the verbs in the box.**

ask	borrow	bring	come	drive	go	~~try~~

A: I (0) ......*'m going to try*..... to get a ticket for the V Festival tonight. Do you want one? The tickets cost £130, with camping. It's a great festival. I went last year.

B: OK, yes, I (1) .... !

A: Brilliant! How many tickets do you want?

B: One. Or maybe two. I (2) .... Lisa to come with me.

A: Do you want two tickets with camping?

B: Yes. We (3) .... a tent from somebody.

A: OK, great. I (4) .... my tent. I bought it last year. I (5) .... there, so you can come with me in my car, if you want.

B: Thanks very much.

A: Well, don't thank me. We haven't got the tickets yet! I (6) .... on their website tonight, so I hope I'm lucky.

55 *I'm leaving at six.*

> I'm **leaving** at six.   He **isn't having** lunch here today.   **Are** you **coming** with us?

We use the present continuous to talk about things we have arranged to do or not to do in the future: *I'm leaving at six.*

 We cannot use *will* to talk about arrangements. We only use it to talk about what we know or think will happen in the future:
You'll feel better tomorrow. (Not ~~You're feeling better tomorrow.~~)

▶▶ **For the form of the present continuous, see Units 37–38.**

P R A C T I C E

55a Complete the conversation. Use the present continuous of the verbs in brackets.

Emma: Can you take me to work on Friday evening, Mum?

Mum: Yes, OK. Dad and I (0) ....*are taking*......... Tom to the station that night, so we can take you to work on the way. (1) .... (Kate / drive) you home that night?

Emma: No. She (2) .... (not work) on Friday.

Mum: Well, I can come and get you. That's OK. Oh, Emma – I've just remembered. What (3) .... (you / do) on Saturday?

Emma: I (4) .... (not do) anything. Why?

Mum: Steve, Anne and their girls (5) .... (come) for lunch.

Emma: Oh, that's nice. And what (6) .... (we / have) for lunch?

Mum: I don't know. Any ideas?

55b Circle the correct answer.

0 I can't come to the cinema because (*I'm meeting*)/*I'll meet* Kim at seven.

1 *They aren't coming /They won't come* with us tomorrow. They're busy.

2 I don't want to talk to Lisa about it. *She isn't listening /She won't listen* to me.

3 *Adam's meeting /Adam will meet* Debbie at eight o'clock tonight.

4 *You're enjoying /You'll enjoy* the film tonight. It's really good.

5 You can leave your books here. *Nobody's taking /Nobody will take* them.

6 Here's our new address. *We're moving /We'll move* next week.

7 *Craig isn't knowing /Craig won't know* the answer. He doesn't know much about computers.

8 *We're going /We'll go* to the concert on Sunday. I've just bought our tickets.

56 *The train leaves at ten.*

> The train **leaves** at ten tonight.   What time **does** it **arrive** tomorrow?

We can use the present simple to talk about the future. We use it to talk about something that is part of a timetable:
*The train **leaves** at ten tonight.* (This is the time in the timetable.)

 We cannot use the present simple to talk about arrangements. We use the present continuous:
I'm meeting Sarah at six tomorrow. (Not *I meet Sarah at six tomorrow.*)

▶▶ **For the form of the present simple, see Units 34–36.**

P R A C T I C E

56a Complete the sentences. Use the present simple of the verbs in brackets.

0 The boat .... *arrives* .... in Dover at six on Monday. (arrive)

1 The last bus .... at eleven. (leave)

2 My new course .... next month. The first day is 6th September. (start)

3 The pool .... at nine tomorrow. (open)

4 The last class .... on Friday. (be)

5 Our plane .... in Kuala Lumpur for four hours. (stop)

6 I can meet you after the play. What time .... ? (it / finish)

7 The post office .... at two tomorrow. (close)

8 What time .... ? (the film / begin)

56b Circle the correct answer.

A: When (0) *do your exams start* / *are your exams starting*?

B: On Thursday. The first one's at nine o'clock.

A: And when (1) *do they finish* / *are they finishing*?

B: On the 17th. And then on the 19th, (2) *I go* / *I'm going* to Scotland with some friends.

A: Lovely! (3) *Do you get* / *Are you getting* the train to Scotland?

B: No, the bus. It's cheaper than the train, but it takes longer. I think that (4) *the bus leaves* / *the bus is leaving* here at seven thirty and (5) *arrives* / *is arriving* in Glasgow at about half past five. (6) *We stay* / *We're staying* the night in Glasgow and (7) *we get* / *we're getting* another bus to Inverness the next morning. (8) *We come* / *We're coming* back on the 21st.

A: I hope you have a great time!

Check 10 Future forms

1 Complete the sentences. Use one word in each gap.

1 I .... not sleep on the plane tomorrow. The seats are too uncomfortable.

2 I .... be tired after the long flight. I was very tired last time.

3 What time .... the plane arrive in London?

4 .... Tom and Isabel going to meet us at the airport?

5 Isabel isn't going .... come. She's at work then.

6 We .... having dinner with her at eight.

7 We aren't .... to hire a car.

8 Isabel .... going to drive us to the hotel after dinner.

/ 8

2 Circle the correct answer.

9 *I'm going to see /I'll see* the doctor tomorrow at ten.

10 *They're performing /They'll perform* their new play on Thursday, Friday and Saturday.

11 *The exhibition finishes /The exhibition's finishing* tomorrow.

12 I can't find a pen, but there's a pencil here. *I'm going to use /I'll use* that.

13 What time *does the film start /is the film starting* tonight?

14 *We're leaving /We'll leave* Rome on Sunday. I've just bought our tickets.

15 *The bank closes /The bank's closing* at eight tomorrow.

/ 7

3 Complete the conversation. Use *will* or *be going* to and the verbs in brackets.

A: I (16) .... (see) Becky on Thursday. Would you like to come too?

B: Yes, I'd love to. Thanks.

A: Great! I (17) .... (tell) Becky.

B: Where (18) .... (you / meet)?

A: I'm not sure. I (19) .... (call) you tomorrow.

B: OK. I've got a new mobile number. I (20) .... (give) it to you now.

/ 5

4 Complete the extract from a letter. Use *will*, the present simple or the present continuous of the verbs in brackets.

The shops (21) .... (open) at half past nine, so we (22) .... (get) a train at about half past eight. It (23) .... (arrive) in London at about a quarter past nine. We (24) .... (have) lunch with Jo at one. I'm sure we (25) .... (have) a great time.

/ 5

Total: / 25

✓ Self-check

Wrong answers	Look again at	Try CD-ROM
4, 5, 7, 8	Unit 52	Exercise 52
1, 2, 25	Unit 53	Exercise 53
9, 12, 16, 17, 18, 19, 20	Unit 54	Exercise 54
6, 10, 14, 22, 24	Unit 55	Exercise 55
3, 11, 13, 15, 21, 23	Unit 56	Exercise 56

Now do **Check 10**

Modal verbs

57 *I can play the guitar.*

> I **can play** the guitar.   Where is he? I **can't see** him.   **Can** you **speak** French?

- We use *can* + infinitive without *to* to talk about something we are able to do:
  - generally: *I **can play** the guitar.*
  - at this moment: *Where is he? I **can't see** him.*
- In negative sentences, we use the short form (*can't*) more often than the full form (*cannot*).

Affirmative	I/you/he/she/it/we/they **can play**
Negative	I/you/he/she/it/we/they **can't (cannot) play**
Question	**Can** I/you/he/she/it/we/they **play**?
Short answers	Yes, I/you/he/she/it/we/they **can**.
	No, I/you/he/she/it/we/they **can't**.

▶▶ *See Appendix 11: Short forms of verbs, page 171.*

PRACTICE

57a Complete the sentences. Use *can* or *can't* and the verbs in brackets.

0   Mark ....*can't sleep*........ . It's four in the morning and he's still watching TV. (sleep)

1   Daniel .... , but he hasn't got a car. (drive)

2   I .... without my glasses. I wear them all the time. (see)

3   What's this film about? I .... it. (understand)

4   Lisa .... with us. She's busy. (come)

5   I spent a year in Madrid, so I .... Spanish now. (speak)

6   I need your help. I .... this box. (carry)

7   He has swimming lessons every week and he .... very well now. (swim)

8   Kate's only ten months old, but she .... (walk)

9   We .... this. We've already spent all our money. (buy)

10 Of course you .... this exercise! It's very easy. (do)

57b **Write questions. Use *can*. Then complete the short answers.**

o you / ride / a bike?
A: *Can you ride a bike?* .... B: Yes, *I can* ....

1 you and Tom / swim?
A: .... B: No, ...

2 Tom / do / karate?
A: .... B: Yes, ...

3 your parents / play / tennis?
A: .... B: No, ...

4 your sister / skate?
A: .... B: No, ...

5 you / run / fast?
A: .... B: Yes, ...

6 you and Tom / ski?
A: .... B: Yes, ...

57c **Write sentences that are true for you. Use *can* or *can't*.**

o read music *I can/can't read music.* ....

1 drive ....

2 cook ....

3 speak Japanese ....

4 play chess ....

5 ride a bike ....

6 swim ....

58 *I could read when I was five.*

| I **could read** when I was five, but I **couldn't write**. **Could** you **write**? |

We use *could* + infinitive without *to* to talk about something we were able to do in the past: *I **could read** when I was five, but I **couldn't write**.*

Affirmative	I/you/he/she/it/we/they **could read**
Negative	I/you/he/she/it/we/they **couldn't (could not) read**
Question	**Could** I/you/he/she/it/we/they **read**?
Short answers	Yes, I/you/he/she/it/we/they **could**.
	No, I/you/he/she/it/we/they **couldn't**.

▶▶ ***See Appendix 11: Short forms of verbs, page 171.***

PRACTICE

58a **Complete the sentences. Use *could* or *couldn't* and the verbs in brackets.**

0 Amy ....*could draw*.......... very well when she was a child. Her pictures were very good. (draw)

1 .... English when she came to London? (Carla / speak)

2 I .... maps when I was younger, but I can now. (read)

3 When we were children, we .... football for hours. We never got tired. (play)

4 .... the sea from your house when you lived in Wales? (you / see)

5 When you were little, you .... my name, so you called me 'Bibi'. (say)

6 My grandfather .... ten kilometres a day when he was seventy. He was very fit. (walk)

7 He's a very clever child. He .... to fifty when he was three. (count)

8 .... a computer when you were six? (you / use)

9 Tommy .... a year ago, but now he can. (swim)

10 .... when she was five? (your sister / write)

58b **Circle the correct answer.**

A: I had a wonderful holiday in Italy when I was a child. I really loved it, but I (0) *can't /couldn't* understand Italian.

B: (1) *Can /Could* your parents speak it?

A: Yes, they (2) *can /could*. They spoke it very well.

A: Nikki wants to play tennis, but I (3) *can't /couldn't* play it at all. (4) *Can /Could* you play?

B: Yes, I (5) *can /could*, but I'm not very good at it. I (6) *can't /couldn't* play at all when I was at school.

A: (7) *Can /Could* you cook, or does your mum do all the cooking?

B: I (8) *can /could* make a few things. My chocolate cake's very good!

A: Wow! Last year you (9) *can't /couldn't* make anything. I remember those biscuits ...

A: (10) *Can /Could* you ride your bike with no hands when you were a child?

B: Yes. My brother taught me. He (11) *can /could* do all kinds of clever things with his bike then, but he (12) *can't /couldn't* do them now. He drives everywhere.

59 *Can I use the car?*

A: **Can I use** the car tomorrow?   B: No, you **can't**. You **can have** it on Sunday.

We use *Can I/we ...?* when we ask for permission to do something. When we give or refuse permission, we use *can/can' t*:
A: **Can I use** the car tomorrow?
B: No, you **can't**. You **can have** it on Sunday morning. But you **can't have** it in the afternoon.

PRACTICE

59a Write questions. Use *can*.

0	I / finish / this tomorrow?	*Can I finish this tomorrow?* ......
1	I / read / your postcard?	......
2	we / leave / our bikes here?	......
3	I / use / your phone?	......
4	I / open / the window?	......
5	we / sit / at that table?	......
6	I / keep / this photo?	......
7	I / tell / her?	......
8	I / look / at your magazine?	......
9	we / put / our tent here?	......
10	we / take / the car?	......

59b Complete the conversations. Use *can* or *can't*.

A: (0) ......*Can*...... I ask you something?
B: Yes, of course you (1) ....
A: (2) .... I borrow your laptop tomorrow?
B: I'm sorry, I need it tomorrow. But you (3) .... use it now if you like.

A: (4) .... we park our car here?
B: No, I'm afraid you (5) .... There's a car park at the end of the street.
A: (6) .... we leave the car there for two or three hours?
B: Yes. You (7) .... leave it there all day.

A: Jess, (8) .... I wear your black skirt on Saturday?
B: I'm sorry, you (9) .... I'm going to wear it to Craig's party. But you (10) .... wear my red dress. You look great in it.
A: Really? Thanks!

60 *We must go.*

> We **must go** now. We **mustn't miss** our plane.
> You **must take** your bag with you. You **mustn't leave** it here.

● We use *must* + infinitive without *to* when we think that something is necessary, or to tell somebody to do something:
  *We **must go** now.   You **must take** your bag with you.*

● We use *mustn't* + infinitive without *to* when we think that it is necessary **not** to do something, or to tell somebody **not** to do something:
  *We **mustn't miss** our plane.   You **mustn't leave** your bag here.*

Affirmative	I/you/he/she/it/we/they **must go**
Negative	I/you/he/she/it/we/they **mustn't** (must not) go

▶▶ **See Appendix 11: Short forms of verbs, page 171.**

PRACTICE

60a Circle the correct answer.

0 I (*must*)/*mustn't* ask Mum for some money. I haven't got enough for my ticket.

1 I *must* /*mustn't* forget to tell Becky. She wants to come, too.

2 We *must* /*mustn't* check the times of the trains again. I'm not sure of them.

3 We *must* /*mustn't* be late for our train.

4 I *must* /*mustn't* take my railcard. I can get cheap tickets with it.

5 You *must* /*mustn't* get the number 7 bus. It doesn't stop at the station.

6 We *must* /*mustn't* lose our tickets. We can't get any more.

60b Complete the rules for an exam. Use *must* or *mustn't* and the verbs in the box.

~~be~~   bring   copy   give   stay   stop   talk   use   write

0 You ....*mustn't be*.......... late for the exam.

1 You .... your mobile phone into the exam.

2 You .... your name at the top of the first page.

3 You .... a pen, not a pencil.

4 During the exam, you .... to anybody.

5 You .... in your chair all the time.

6 You .... another person's answers.

7 You .... when I say, 'Stop now'.

8 You .... me your answer sheet at the end of the exam.

61 *I have to go.*

> I **have to go** now.　　We **don't have to walk** home.　　**Does** he **have to do** this now?

- We use *have to* + infinitive to say that something is necessary:
  *I **have to go** now. It's late.*

- We use *don't have to* + infinitive to say that something is not necessary:
  *We **don't have to walk** home. We can take the bus.*

- We can use *have* to like *must*: *I **have to go** now. / I **must go** now.*
- But *don't have to* and *mustn't* are different. Compare:
  *You **don't have to stay** here.* (It is not necessary, but you can if you want to.)
  *You **mustn't stay** here.* (Do not stay here. You must leave.)

Affirmative	
I/you/we/they **have to go**	he/she/it **has to go**
Negative	
I/you/we/they **don't** (**do not**) have to go	he/she/it **doesn't** (**does not**) have to go
Question	
Do I/you/we/they **have to go**?	**Does** he/she/it **have to go**?

PRACTICE

61a Complete the sentences. Use *have/has to* or *don't/doesn't have to*.

0 I ......*don't have to*...... go to college today. I haven't got any lectures.

1 You can't take your bags into the museum. You .... leave them here.

2 Jack .... get the bus to town. He can't walk there.

3 We can get the tickets tomorrow. We .... buy them now.

4 You .... answer my question now. You can tell me later.

5 My dad .... stay in hospital today and tomorrow. He can come out on Monday.

6 My sister .... wear glasses. Her eyes are fine.

7 I .... earn some money for my holiday. I haven't got any.

8 He .... work. He's got a lot of money.

9 No, I'm afraid I can't come with you. I .... finish this project today.

10 You .... wash the car. Dan washed it yesterday.

61b **Write questions. Use *have to*.**

o what / we / do / this weekend?   *What do we have to do this weekend?*

1 we / visit / anybody?   ....

2 you / call / Lisa?   ....

3 why / Ben / have / the car?   ....

4 I / help / him and Sarah?   ....

5 they / leave / early on Sunday?   ....

6 where / Sarah / go?   ....

7 we / get / any petrol?   ....

8 you / work / on your project?   ....

61c **Complete the conversation. Use the correct form of *have to*.**

A: When (o) ....*do we have to*............ (we) check in at the airport tomorrow?

B: Two hours before the flight – at about six. So we (1) ....
get the bus at about four.

A: I'm going to change some money this afternoon.

B: You (2) .... change it today. You can change it at the
airport.

A: Yes, that's true. Have you packed yet?

B: No. I (3) .... do that this evening. This afternoon, I'm
helping Jonathan with his car. He (4) .... fix it today
because he needs it tomorrow. He's going to see Hannah in Manchester. He
(5) .... drive there, but it's easier than going by train or
bus.

B: (6) .... (he) go tomorrow?

A: Yes. They're going to a party together in the evening.

61d **Circle the correct answer.**

o We (mustn't)/ *don't have to* be late for the bus. It's the last one.

1 We *mustn't* / *don't have to* run. We can walk.

2 I *mustn't* / *don't have to* lose Emma's address. I need it.

3 You *mustn't* / *don't have to* pay for my ticket. I've got enough money.

4 I *mustn't* / *don't have to* forget my camera tomorrow.

5 I *mustn't* / *don't have to* miss my bus stop. I don't want to walk a long way.

6 We *mustn't* / *don't have to* phone Jessica now. We can call her tomorrow.

7 You *mustn't* / *don't have to* bring any food tomorrow. I'll bring some.

8 You *mustn't* / *don't have to* leave your coat on the bus.

Check 11 Modal verbs (1)

1 Complete the conversations. Use *can, can't, could* **or** *couldn't.*

A: (1) .... I ask you something?

B: Sure. What?

A: (2) .... you play in the street when you were a child?

B: No, it was too busy.

A: Are you leaving?

B: Yes. I'm sorry – we (3) .... stay.

A: (4) .... we sit on the balcony?

B: Yes. There are some chairs over there.

A: Why are you tired?

B: I (5) .... sleep last night. It was too hot.

/ 5

2 Circle the correct answer.

6 You *mustn't / don't have to* use your mobile phone on the plane. It's dangerous.

7 This course isn't free. You *have to / don't have to* pay for it.

8 I *must / mustn't* get some batteries for my radio. I haven't got any.

9 Sam *mustn't / doesn't have to* take us to the airport. We can go by bus.

10 We *must / mustn't* forget our passports.

/ 5

3 Complete the conversation. Use the verbs in the box.

can   can't   don't have to   must   mustn't

A: Are you ready?

B: Yes. Oh – I (11) .... get my camera. (12) .... I put it in your bag?

B: Sure. Where's my bag? I (13) .... find it.

A: It's here – with your keys. You (14) .... go without them.

B: Have you got any money for the bus?

A: We (15) .... get the bus. We can walk.

/ 5

4 Complete the extract from a magazine article. Use *can, can't, could* **or** *couldn't* **and the verbs in the box.**

dance   learn   play   practise   read

When I was a child, I didn't like books. I (16) .... them easily. I loved dance and music. I (17) .... different dance steps very quickly, and I (18) .... the piano.

I love dancing now, too. I (19) .... for hours. I sometimes play the piano at my friend's house, but I (20) .... at home because we haven't got a piano.

/ 5

Total: / 20

✓ Self-check

Wrong answers	Look again at	Try CD-ROM
3, 13, 19, 20	Unit 57	Exercise 57
2, 5, 16, 17, 18	Unit 58	Exercise 58
1, 4, 12	Unit 59	Exercise 59
8, 10, 11, 14	Unit 60	Exercise 60
6, 7, 9, 15	Unit 61	Exercise 61

Now do **Check 11**

62 *Can/Could you help me?*

Can you help me?   **Could you speak** more slowly, please?

- We use *Can/Could you* + infinitive without *to* when we ask somebody to do something for us: **Can you help** me?   **Could you speak** more slowly, please?

⚠ *Could you ...?* is more formal and polite than *Can you ...?*

P R A C T I C E

62a Re-write the sentences. Use *Could you*.

0	Put this in the bin.	*Could you put this in the bin?*
1	Sign this card.	....
2	Move your chair.	....
3	Meet me at the station.	....
4	Turn off the TV.	....
5	Wait for me.	....
6	Hold this for a minute.	....
7	Give him my message.	....
8	Open the door.	....

62b Complete the sentences. Use *Can/Could you* and the verbs in the box.

ask   close   drive   get   give   ~~lend~~   say

0 You haven't got enough money for a sandwich.
   You ask Tom, '.....*Could you lend*....... me the money for a sandwich, please?'

1 You're cold and Tom's sitting by the window.
   You ask him, '...................................... the window, please?'

2 Tom's going to buy some tickets for a concert.
   You ask him, '...................................... a ticket for me, too, please?'

3 You've got a book for Mark.
   You ask Tom, '...................................... this to Mark, please?'

4 Tom says something but you don't understand it.
   You ask him, '...................................... that again, please?'

5 You have to be at the airport in half an hour. Tom's got a car.
   You ask him, '...................................... me to the airport, please?'

6 You're interested in working in a bank. Tom's father works in a bank.
   You ask him, '...................................... your dad about that job in his bank, please?'

63 *I'll help you. / Shall I help you?*

I'**ll help** you with that suitcase.   **Shall I drive** him to the airport?

We can use *I' ll ...* and *Shall I ...?* when we offer to do something for somebody:
A: *I can' t carry this suitcase.*   B: *I'**ll help** you.*
A: *His plane leaves at six.*   B: ***Shall I drive** him to the airport?*

P R A C T I C E

63a **Complete the conversations. Use *I'll* and the verbs in the box.**

| bring   buy   ~~draw~~   make   mend   phone   show |

o **A:** I don't know the way to the station.   **B:** ....*I'll draw*.......... a map for you.

1 **A:** We need to arrange to meet Lucy.   **B:** .... her tonight.

2 **A:** There's a hole in my sleeping bag.   **B:** .... it for you.

3 **A:** We need some music for the journey.   **B:** .... my MP3 player.

4 **A:** I don't know how to put up a tent.   **B:** .... you.

5 **A:** I haven't bought the tickets yet.   **B:** .... them tomorrow.

6 **A:** We need some food.   **B:** .... some sandwiches.

63b **Write questions. Use *Shall I*. Then match the questions to sentences a–g.**

a **A:** I don't feel well. ☐

b **A:** I'm going home now. ☐

c **A:** Our train arrives at ten. ☐ *o*

d **A:** It's hot in here. ☐

e **A:** I need to speak to Simon. ☐

f **A:** We need some washing powder. ☐

g **A:** It's very dark in here! ☐

> Shall I meet you at the station?

o meet / you at the station?   **B:** *Shall I meet you at the station?* ....

1 get / you some aspirin?   **B:** ....

2 go / to the supermarket?   **B:** ....

3 open / the window?   **B:** ....

4 come / with you?   **B:** ....

5 turn on / the light?   **B:** ....

6 ask / him to phone you?   **B:** ....

63c **Complete the sentences. Use *I'll* or *Shall I* and the verbs in the box.**

| bring | carry | drive | give | ~~lend~~ | make | turn on | show | wash |

o A: I need a guidebook to Italy. B: I've got one. I ....*'ll lend*.......... it to you.

1 A: Have you got any good CDs? B: Yes. .... some to the party?

2 A: Are all the cups dirty? B: Yes. .... them?

3 A: I need Jo's e-mail address. B: .... it to you.

4 A: How does this camera work? B: Wait. .... you.

5 A: I'm tired. B: .... your bag for you?

6 A: I'm hungry. B: .... an omelette.

7 A: I'm late. B: .... you to the station.

8 A: I want to listen to the news. B: .... the radio?

64 *Let's go to the beach.*

We can make suggestions in different ways:

Let's + infinitive without *to*	***Let's go*** to the beach.
Shall we + infinitive without *to*	***Shall we take*** some food?
Why don't we + infinitive without *to*	***Why don't we make*** some sandwiches?
What about + *-ing*	***What about buying*** some fruit?
How about + *-ing*	***How about getting*** some coffee?

PRACTICE

64a **Complete the sentences. Use *Let's* or *Shall we* and the verbs in brackets.**

o ....*Shall we go*.......... home now? (go)

1 .... some chocolate. (buy)

2 .... a taxi? (get)

3 .... up this street. (walk)

4 .... for the bus. (wait)

5 .... some coffee? (have)

6 .... Philip and Sarah to come with us? (ask)

7 .... Adam to the party. (invite)

8 .... to some music? (listen)

64b **Complete the conversation. Use *why don't we* or *how about*.**

A: (0) ...... *Why don't we* ...... eat out tonight?

B: OK. (1) .... having a pizza?

A: Sure. (2) .... try that new pizzeria in King Street?

B: Or (3) .... going to the one near the shopping centre?

A: OK. (4) .... meet there at eight?

B: Great! Listen, (5) .... asking Leanne to come, too?

A: Yes, that's a great idea! (6) .... call her now?

B: OK. I'll call her. See you later then!

64c **Circle the correct answer.**

A: (0) *Why don't we* / *What about* watch a DVD?

B: OK. (1) *Let's* / *Shall we* watch this James Bond one.
_____

A: (2) *Let's* / *What about* having a party next Saturday?

B: Great! (3) *Let's* / *Shall we* invite everyone from college?

A: Sure. (4) *Why don't we* / *How about* send everyone an e-mail now?
_____

A: (5) *Why don't we* / *What about* go shopping together tomorrow?

B: Yes, that's a good idea. (6) *Let's* / *Shall we* meet at ten?
_____

A: (7) *Let's* / *How about* going to the cinema tonight?

B: OK. What's on?

A: I don't know. (8) *Why don't we* / *Let's* look in the newspaper.
_____

A: (9) *Why don't we* / *How about* listening to some music?

B: Sure. I bought this great CD last week. (10) *Let's* / *Shall we* listen to it.

65 *You should stay.*

You **should stay**.	You **shouldn't leave** now.	What **should** I **do**?

- We use *should* + infinitive without *to* to give advice:
  *You **should stay**.   You **shouldn't leave** now.*
- We use the question form to ask for advice: *What **should** I **do**?*

Affirmative	I/you/he/she/it/we/they **should stay**
Negative	I/you/he/she/it/we/they **shouldn't (should not) stay**
Question	**Should** I/you/he/she/it/we/they **stay**?
Short answers	Yes, I/you/he/she/it/we/they **should**.
	No, I/you/he/she/it/we/they **shouldn't**.

▶▶ *See Appendix 11: Short forms of verbs, page 171.*

P R A C T I C E

65a **Complete the sentences. Use** *should* **or** *shouldn't* **and the verbs in brackets.**

0 You look tired. You ....*should go*..................... to bed. (go)

1 You .... about your exams. You'll be all right. (worry)

2 You .... him the truth. (tell)

3 You're always late for class! You .... earlier. (get up)

4 You .... to him. He doesn't know everything! (listen)

5 You .... so much sugar. It's bad for you. (eat)

6 It's cold outside. You .... a coat. (wear)

65b **Lucy is having dinner with some Japanese friends tomorrow. She is asking another Japanese friend for advice. Complete her questions. Use** *should.*

~~be~~   buy   eat   greet   leave   sit   wear

0 ....*Should I be*................... there before six?

1 What .... ? Are jeans all right?

2 .... a present?

3 How .... people?

4 .... everything on my plate?

5 How .... on the floor?

6 What time .... ?

65c **Complete the sentences. Use** *You should* **or** *You shouldn't* **and the verbs in the box.**

~~do~~   drink   eat   get   go   sleep   work

HOW TO STAY HEALTHY

✱ (0) ....*You should do*............. some exercise every day.

✱ (1) .... lots of fruit and vegetables.

✱ (2) .... a lot of coffee.

✱ (3) .... for about eight hours every night.

✱ (4) .... to bed late.

✱ (5) .... for a long time without a break.

✱ (6) .... some fresh air every day.

66 *She may/might be at home.*

> She **may/might be** at home.   I **may/might not go** to London tomorrow.

We use *may* or *might* + infinitive without *to* to talk about things that are possible now or in the future:
She **may/might be** at home.   Paul **may/might have** your keys.
She **may/might not come** with us.   I **may/might not go** to London tomorrow.

Affirmative	I/you/he/she/it/we/they **may/might come**
Negative	I/you/he/she/it/we/they **may/might not come**

⚠ *Mightn't* is the short form of *might not*. There is not a short form of *may not*.

▶▶ **See Appendix 11: Short forms of verbs, page 171.**

PRACTICE

66a Re-write the sentences. Use *may* or *may not*.

0   It's possible that it will rain tomorrow.   *It may rain tomorrow.*

1   It's possible that we won't go to the beach.   ....

2   It's possible that Ryan will come here.   ....

3   It's possible that my parents won't be here.   ....

4   It's possible that we'll watch a DVD.   ....

5   It's possible that James will join us.   ....

6   It's possible that we won't stay at home.   ....

7   It's possible that we'll go to the cinema.   ....

8   It's possible that James won't come with us.   ....

66b Complete the conversation. Use *may* or *might* and the verbs in brackets.

A: Shall we phone this hotel and book some rooms?
B: Yes, but let's choose another hotel, too. Their rooms (0) .... *might be* .... (be) too expensive, or they (1) .... (not have) enough rooms.
A: How about this one? In fact, Hannah (2) .... (prefer) this one.
B: Yes, but Emily (3) .... (not like) it. It's more old-fashioned.
A: Let's ask Sarah. She (4) .... (know) a good hotel. She lived in Brighton for two years.
B: Good idea. Is she coming to the wedding?
A: Yes, she is. But she (5) .... (not stay) in a hotel. She (6) .... (stay) with a friend.

Check 12 Modal verbs (2)

1 Circle the correct answer.

A: (1) *Shall / Let's* we play tennis tomorrow?

B: Oh, yes. That's a good idea.

A: (2) *Should / May* I book a court?

B: Yes, they're all very busy. You need to book one.

A: OK. (3) *I'll / Shall I* phone them now. (4) *Should / Could* you bring some tennis balls?

B: Sure. And (5) *can / might* you book a court for Wednesday, too?

A: Yes, fine.

/ 5

2 Complete the sentences. Use the verbs in brackets and the verbs in the box.

drink go put sit take

6 .... here for a few minutes. (let's)

7 When it's hot, you .... a lot of water. (should)

8 .... you .... this to the kitchen? (can)

9 Natalie .... to Portugal next summer. (might)

10 .... I .... these biscuits in the cupboard? (shall)

/ 5

3 Complete the conversations. Use one word in each gap.

11 A: How .... going to the cinema tonight?

B: Yes, that's a good idea. What's on?

12 A: I've got a headache.

B: .... I get you some aspirin?

13 A: Are you coming tomorrow?

B: I don't know. I .... not have time.

14 A: My plants are dying.

B: You should .... leave them in the sun. It's too hot for them.

15 A: .... you move your suitcase, please?

B: Sure.

/ 5

4 Re-write the sentences.

16 Let's listen to some music.
How .... to some music?

17 Shall I make some sandwiches?
I .... some sandwiches.

18 It's possible that it isn't here.
It .... here.

19 Let's look in this drawer.
Why don't .... in this drawer?

20 It's possible that Mark has it.
Mark .... it.

/ 5

Total: / 20

Statements

67 *I like it. It's nice.*

In English, the order of the words in statements is:

Subject	Verb
Mark	is coming.
She	stopped.

Subject	Verb	Object
Laura	has got	a car.
I	like	it.

Subject	Verb	Adverb
They	play	well.
Tom	lives	here.
He	is leaving	now.

Subject	Verb *(be)*	Adjective
It	is	nice.
The boys	were	tired.

▶▶ *For the position of adverbs of frequency in statements, see Unit 31.*

PRACTICE

67a **Write the sentences in the box in the correct group.**

> The tickets were expensive.   We were amazed.
> The music was fantastic.   Kate smiled.
> We loved it.   She liked the songs.
> A man sang.   My brother was there.
> He sang beautifully.   I bought the CD.
> Everybody listened carefully.   We left.

Subject	Verb

Subject	Verb	Object

Subject	Verb	Adverb

Subject	Verb	Adjective
The tickets	*were*	*expensive.*

67b **Put the words in the correct order.**

0 him / I / don't know .... *I don't know him.* ....

1 she / a sandwich / didn't want ....

2 tomorrow / our exams / start ....

3 everybody / hard / worked ....

4 are having / a party / they ....

5 spoke / we / quietly ....

6 ill / was / Ryan ....

7 arrived / yesterday / my cousins ....

8 his coat / he / forgot ....

68 *I gave Joe a book. / I gave a book to Joe.*

Some verbs can have two objects. Some of these verbs are: *bring, buy, get, give, lend, make, offer, send, show, teach, write.* We can use two different structures with these verbs:

Subject	Verb	Object (person)	Object (thing)
I	gave	Joe	a book.
I	bought	Emma	a present.

Subject	Verb	Object (thing)	*to/for*	Object (person)
I	gave	a book	to	Joe.
I	bought	a present	for	Emma.

⚠ We use *to* + object after *bring, give, lend, offer, send, show, teach* and *write*. We use *for* + object after *buy, get* and *make*.

P R A C T I C E

68a **Complete the sentences. Write the words in brackets in the correct place.**

0 I lent .... *Rachel* .... my camera .... for her trip. (Rachel)

1 She sent .... me .... from Paris. (a postcard)

2 She brought .... some French chocolate .... (Jo)

3 She showed .... her photos .... (us)

4 She gave .... me .... (a ring)

5 And she bought .... Jo .... for her birthday. (a present)

6 She taught .... some French words .... (us)

68b **Put the words in the correct order.**

0 some tea / made / I've / us   *I've made us some tea.*

1 brought / your book / I've / you   ....

2 offered / some cake / me / Sam   ....

3 me / they / some money / gave   ....

4 a CD / I / Sarah / bought   ....

5 we / Becky / sent / a letter   ....

6 lent / his jacket / Adam / me   ....

7 my photos / you / show / I'll   ....

8 you / a ticket / I / got   ....

68c **Dan moved to Spain last month. He gave some of his things to his friends. Look at the table and complete the sentences. Use object + *to* + object.**

Kirsty	Matt	me	Nikki	Jamie	Rob	Lisa
0	1	2	3	4	5	6

0 He gave *his lamp to Kirsty.* ....

1 He gave ....

2 He gave ....

3 He gave ....

4 He gave ....

5 He gave ....

6 He gave ....

68d **Re-write the sentences. Use *to* or *for* where necessary.**

0 Paul wrote his friend a letter.   *Paul wrote a letter to his friend.*

1 I've bought him a CD.   ....

2 We got some earrings for Kelly.   ....

3 I'm sending a text message to Tim.   ....

4 Lucy's made us a cake.   ....

5 We gave the waitress a big tip.   ....

6 Mark showed his new bike to Alex.   ....

7 They offered Jess £1,000.   ....

8 Bring that book to me.   ....

69 *Wait here. Don't go.*

> **Wait** here.   **Don't go** anywhere.   **Mind** your head!   **Don't** move!

- We use the imperative to:
  - tell somebody to do something: **Wait** here.   **Don't go** anywhere.
  - warn somebody: **Mind** your head!   **Don't move**!
  - give instructions and directions: **Press** this button.   **Turn** left.
  - offer something to somebody: **Have** a biscuit.
  - give somebody good wishes: **Have** a good day.
- We often use *please* with the imperative, when we want to be more polite:
  Sit here, please.
- To form the imperative, we use the infinitive without *to*. To form negative
  sentences, we use *don't* (*do not*) + infinitive without *to*:
  Stop.   **Don't stop**.

P R A C T I C E

69a **Complete the sentences. Use the imperative of the verbs in brackets. Use full forms.**

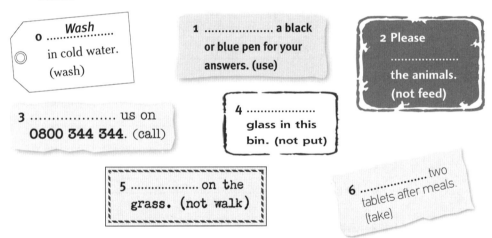

0 ......*Wash*...... in cold water. (wash)

1 .... a black or blue pen for your answers. (use)

2 Please .... the animals. (not feed)

3 .... us on 0800 344 344. (call)

4 .... glass in this bin. (not put)

5 .... on the grass. (not walk)

6 .... two tablets after meals. (take)

69b **Complete the sentences. Use the imperative of the verbs in the box.**

> come   ~~have~~   not forget   not go   not tell   say   take

0 Bye! ......*Have*...... a nice weekend!

1 .... without your map. You'll need it.

2 Here – .... this sandwich. You might get hungry.

3 .... your camera. You'll need that, too.

4 .... hello to Beth for me.

5 .... her about the party. It's a surprise.

6 .... for lunch on Wednesday. I'm free then.

70 *There's a CD near the computer.*

We use *there is/there are* to say that something or somebody exists.

Singular	
Affirmative	**There's** a CD near the computer.
Negative	**There isn't** any money in your purse.
Question	**Is there** a phone here?
Short answers	Yes, **there is.** / No, **there isn't.**

Plural	
Affirmative	**There are** some DVDs on the shelf.
Negative	**There aren't** any batteries in your MP3 player.
Question	**Are there** any messages for me?
Short answers	Yes, **there are.** / No, **there aren't.**

PRACTICE

70a **Look at the map and complete the sentences. Use *there's/there are* or *there isn't/there aren't.***

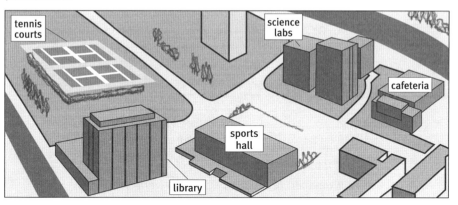

0 In this part of the college, ...*there's*........... a sports hall.

1 And .... three science labs.

2 .... a swimming pool.

3 .... any offices.

4 .... a cafeteria.

5 .... any music practice rooms.

6 .... a business school.

7 .... two tennis courts.

8 And .... a library.

70b Complete the questions. Use *is there* or *are there*.

0 ....*Are there*.......... any showers at the beach?

1 .... a bottle of water in the car?

2 .... any sandwiches in that bag?

3 .... more towels in the car?

4 .... any sun cream?

5 .... a hat in the car?

6 How much orange juice .... ?

70c Complete the conversation. Use the correct form of *there is/there are*.

A: (0) ....*Are there*.......... any good restaurants near here?

B: No, (1) .... (2) .... a very nice one in Westfield, but that's five kilometres from here.

A: (3) .... a bus to Westfield?

B: Yes, (4) .... Do you want to go there?

A: Yes. I'd like to have a nice meal and go shopping.

B: Well, Westfield's a small town. (5) .... any big shops – just small ones.

A: That's OK. (6) .... any clothes shops or sports shops?

B: (7) .... a few clothes shops but (8) .... a sports shop.

A: OK, never mind. I can go to a sports shop in Brighton.

71   *It's raining.*

It's raining.   It's half past eleven.   It was dark.

We use *it* to talk about:

● the weather: ***It's** raining.*   ***It was warm yesterday.***

● the time: ***It's** half past eleven.*   ***It's** late.*

● days: ***It's** Friday.*   ***It's** the 12th of June.*   *Is **it** the last day of your holiday today?*

● distance: ***It's** a long way to the bus stop.*   *How far is **it** to the town centre?*

● the conditions around us: ***It's** nice here.*   ***It** was dark.*

⚠   We do not use *there* and *it* in the same way. Compare:
***There's** a black cloud above the mountain.*   ***It's** cloudy.*

▶▶   **For *'there is/there isn't'*, see Unit 70.**

PRACTICE

71a **Complete the sentences. Use *it's*, *it isn't* or *is it*.**

0 ....*It's*........ late. Everybody's in bed.

1 I can't hear anything. .... very quiet.

2 .... dark. The sun is up.

3 How far .... from here to the college?

4 .... Jack's birthday today. I've just bought him a present.

5 What time .... ? I have to call Nina at eight.

6 .... far from here to the station. I can walk there in five minutes.

7 What day .... today?

8 .... cold. You won't need your jacket.

71b **Complete the answers. Use *it* and the words in brackets.**

0 **A:** Did it rain on Sunday?   **B:** No, but ....*it was cloudy*.................. . (cloudy)

1 **A:** Did you walk here?   **B:** Yes. .... ! (a long way)

2 **A:** Is it eleven o'clock?   **B:** No. .... (midnight)

3 **A:** What's the date today?   **B:** .... (the 22nd)

4 **A:** Was it windy on the boat?   **B:** No, ... (fine)

5 **A:** Was it cold yesterday?   **B:** No, but .... (wet)

6 **A:** Was it light at six?   **B:** No, ... (still dark)

7 **A:** Do you have to leave?   **B:** Yes. .... (late)

8 **A:** I like it here.   **B:** Yes, ... (nice)

71c **Circle the correct answer.**

A: (0) (*It's*)/ *There's* very hot outside!

B: I know. (1) *It's* / *There's* some cold water in the fridge. Do you want some?

A: Yes, please. (2) *It's* / *There's* nice in here. Nice and cool!

A: (3) *It's* / *There's* a good programme on Channel 4 at eight.

B: Really? What time (4) *is it* / *is there* now?

A: (5) *It's* / *There's* quarter to eight.

A: (6) *It's* / *There's* a message for you from Rob on the phone.

B: Thanks. (7) *It's* / *There's* his birthday on the 9th and he's having a party. I've got some CDs for it. (8) *It's* / *There's* a shop in town that sells cheap CDs and I got them there.

A: Yeah. I know that shop. It's really good.

Check 13 Statements

1 Put the words in the correct order.

1 talking / we / loudly / weren't

....

2 Jack / a bike / hasn't got

....

3 her new phone / she / me / showed

....

4 the train / late / was

....

5 not / do / on the grass / walk

....

| / 5 |

2 Complete the conversation. Use one word in each gap.

A: How far is (6) .... to the swimming pool from here?

B: About a kilometre. There (7) .... a bus that can take you to the swimming pool, but you can walk there, too. It isn't far.

A: Which way do I go?

B: Turn right at the traffic lights. (8) .... not cross the road. (9) ....'s a big furniture shop round the corner. The swimming pool's next to it. It might be crowded today because (10) ....'s Sunday.

A: I don't mind. Thanks very much.

| / 5 |

3 Circle the correct answer.

11 *There's / There are* some grapes in the fridge.

12 *There's / It's* half past two.

13 Are *they / there* any spoons in that drawer?

14 *There isn't / There aren't* a film on television this evening.

15 *Don't / Not* leave your shoes there.

| / 5 |

4 Complete the conversation. Write the words in brackets in the correct place.

A: It's Anna's birthday tomorrow. Have you (16) .... bought .... anything? (her)

B: I got (17) .... these earrings for .... yesterday. (her)

A: Oh, they're beautiful. I (18) .... love .... ! (them)

B: I'm going to give (19) .... to her .... in the morning. (them)

A: I'm going to give (20) .... her .... (a CD)

| / 5 |

| Total: | / 20 |

✓ **Self-check**

Wrong answers	Look again at	Try CD-ROM
1, 2, 4, 18	**Unit 67**	Exercise 67
3, 16, 17, 19, 20	**Unit 68**	Exercise 68
5, 8, 15	**Unit 69**	Exercise 69
7, 9, 11, 13, 14	**Unit 70**	Exercise 70
6, 10, 12	**Unit 71**	Exercise 71

Now do **Check 13**

Questions

72 Are you leaving?

Are you leaving?	Does Sam know?	Can I help?

Yes/No questions (= questions that we can answer with *yes* or *no*) begin with an auxiliary verb (*be, have, do*) or a modal verb (e.g. *can, should, will*). We put the subject after the auxiliary/modal verb.

You	are	leaving.	I	can	help
Are	you	leaving?	Can	I	help?

	Sam	knows.		She	won.
Does	Sam	know?	Did	she	win?

⚠ *Have they got a big flat?* (Not *Have got they a big flat?*)
Was Jack working at eight? (Not *Was working Jack at eight?*)

P R A C T I C E

72a Put the words in the correct order.

0 watching / the match / they / are?
Are they watching the match?

1 anything / do / need / you? ....

2 you / open / the window / could? ....

3 have / gone / they / with Adam? ....

4 to / you / stay here / are / going? ....

5 borrow / can / this book / I? ....

6 he / did / a message / leave? ....

7 will / full / be / the campsite? ....

8 got / a dog / they / have? ....

9 you / talking / to me / are? ....

10 she / for you / waiting / was? ....

72b **Write questions.**

0 Luke and Ben are arriving at ten.   *Are Luke and Ben arriving at ten?*

1 Luke's staying with Jack.   ....

2 Jack can take him to the match.   ....

3 You've met Luke.   ....

4 He's Kate's brother.   ....

5 He lives in Cambridge.   ....

6 He and Jack were at the same school.   ....

72c **Complete the conversation. Use the correct form of the verbs in brackets.**

A: (0) ....*Does Sarah go*......... (Sarah / go) to the same college as you?

B: Yes, she does. I often see her.

A: (1) .... (you / do) the same subjects?

B: Yes. Well, we do Computer Studies together.

A: (2) .... (you / see) her yesterday?

B: No. I didn't go to college yesterday. (3) .... (she / phone) you last night about the cinema?

A: Yes, but I can't go. I'm going out with Jessica. (4) .... (you / know) her? Jessica Simpson?

B: Um ... maybe. (5) .... (she / come) to your party last week?

A: Yes. She's got long dark hair and she was wearing a green top and jeans.

B: Yes, I remember her. (6) .... (she / work) in a clothes shop?

A: Yes, she does. She's been there for about a year.

72d **Complete the questions. Then do the quiz. Write answers that are true for you.**

Quiz: Are you happy?

- (0) ....*Do you live*......... in a nice place? (you / live)   *Yes, I do.*

- (1) .... your course/job? (you / like)   ....

- (2) .... a holiday every year? (you / have)   ....

- (3) .... a lot of friends? (you / have got)   ....

- (4) .... a lot of time with them? (you / spend)   ....

- (5) .... near you? (they / live)   ....

- (6) .... friends easily? (you / make)   ....

73   *When are you leaving?*

When are you leaving?   **Where** are you going?   **How often** do you go there?

- *Wh-* questions begin with a question word (e.g. *when, where, why*). After the question word, we use the same word order as in *yes/no* questions.
- We use:
  - *when* to ask about time: **When** *did you get here?*
  - *where* to ask about places: **Where** *are you going?*
  - *why* to ask about the reason for something: **Why** *were you late?*
  - *how* to ask about the way to do something: **How** *do I get to town?*
  - *how much/how many* to ask about quantity:
    How much *money have you got?*   **How many** *eggs do we need?*
- We also use *how* to ask about somebody's health: **How** *are you?*
- We can use *how* + adjective/adverb to ask about degree:
  How tall *are you?*   **How often** *do you go there?*

▶▶ *For 'yes/no' questions, see Unit 72. For when to use 'how much' or 'how many', see Unit 7. For more question words, see Unit 74.*

P R A C T I C E

73a **Circle the correct answer.**

  0 **A:** *How /(Where)* do you live?
  B: In London.

  1 **A:** *And where /why* do you go to college?
  B: I go to Southgate.

  2 **A:** *How /When* did you start there?
  B: Last year.

  3 **A:** *Why /When* did you choose to go there?
  B: Because I liked the place and the course.

  4 **A:** *How /When* do you get there?
  B: I usually go by bus.

  5 **A:** And *why /when* are you doing a tourism course?
  B: Because I want to be a hotel manager.

  6 **A:** *Where /How* do you become a hotel manager?
  B: You have to work in hotels first.

  7 **A:** *Where /How* have you worked?
  B: At the President and at the Hampton Inn.

  8 **A:** *How /When*'s your next exam?
  B: In March.

73b **Complete the questions. Use *where, when, why* or *how*.**

0   A: ....*When*........ did you have lunch?   B: At half past one.

1   A: .... is he leaving?   B: Because he's tired.

2   A: ....'s Lucy?   B: She's fine, thanks.

3   A: .... are you going?   B: To the park.

4   A: .... do I turn this on?   B: Press that green button.

5   A: .... are they coming?   B: Tomorrow.

6   A: .... do you need £100?   B: I want to buy that dress.

7   A: ....'s your birthday?   B: On 18th August.

8   A: .... much time have we got?   B: Ten minutes.

9   A: .... were you late last night?   B: Because I missed my bus.

10 A: ....'s Lisa?   B: She's in her room.

73c **Big Ben is the name of the bell in a famous clock tower in London. Complete the questions about it. Use *how* and the words in the box.**

| big   heavy   high   many   often   ~~old~~   wide |

0   A: ....*How old*........ is the bell?   B: About 150 years old.

1   A: .... is it?   B: 13,760 kilograms.

2   A: .... does it ring?   B: Every hour.

3   A: .... clock faces are there?   B: Four.

4   A: .... is each clock face?   B: More than 7 m wide.

5   A: .... are the numbers on the clocks?   B: About 61 cm long.

6   A: .... is the clock tower?   B: 97 metres.

73d **Ryan is asking Lee about his new car. Write his questions.**

0   where / you / get / your car?   *Where did you get your car?*

1   how / you / find/ it?   ....

2   when / you / get / it?   ....

3   how much / it / cost?   ....

4   why / you / choose / this car?   ....

5   how old / it / be?   ....

6   how fast / it / go?   ....

7   how big / the engine / be?   ....

8   how much petrol / it / use?   ....

9   why / you / need / a car?   ....

10 how often / you / use / it?   ....

74 *Who did you phone?*

> **Who** did you phone?   **What** did he say?   **What time** are you going?
> **Which** bus are you getting?   **Whose** sunglasses are these?

- We use *who* to ask about people: ***Who** did you phone?*
- We use *what* to ask about things. We can use a noun after *what*:
  ***What** did he say?*   ***What time** are you going?*
- We use *which* to ask about things or people. We can use it with or without a noun:
  ***Which** bus are you getting?*   ***Which** is better? This one or that one?*
- We use *whose* to ask about possession. We can use it with or without a noun:
  ***Whose** sunglasses are these?*   ***Whose** is this?*

⚠ We normally use *which* when there are only a few possible answers, and *what* when there are a lot of possible answers. Compare:
***Which** colour do you prefer – black or blue?*   ***What** colour is your new dress?*

▶▶ *For 'yes/no' questions, see Unit 72. For more question words, see Unit 73.*

P R A C T I C E

74a **Complete the questions. Use *who, what, which* or *whose*.**

0	A: ......*Whose*...... is this phone?	B: It's Kirsty's, I think.
1	A: ....'s that girl's name?	B: Emma.
2	A: ....'s in the kitchen?	B: Danielle.
3	A: .... are Craig's keys?	B: Those on the blue keyring.
4	A: .... has Sarah invited?	B: Lots of people from college.
5	A: .... are these photos?	B: They might be Jenny's.
6	A: .... is nicer? This one or that one?	B: This one.

74b **Complete the questions. Use *what* and the words in the box.**

> books   colour   day   kind (x2)   size   ~~time~~

0	A: ......*What time*...... did you get home?	B: At half past five.
1	A: .... is your new jacket?	B: Black.
2	A: .... are your shoes?	B: Thirty eight.
3	A: .... of juice would you like?	B: Orange juice, please.
4	A: .... did you buy?	B: These two about Spain.
5	A: .... is it today?	B: Friday.
6	A: .... of ice cream would you like?	B: Vanilla, please.

74c Circle the correct answer.

0 *What /* (*Which*) glass is yours? This one or that one?

1 *What /Which* kind of films does Rob like?

2 *What /Which* one is the cheapest?

3 *What /Which* time are they coming?

4 *What /Which* cake are you having? The lemon or the coffee?

5 *What /Which* colour is Lisa's car?

6 *What /Which* T-shirt did she buy? The red one or the black one?

74d Complete the questions. Use one word in each space. Do you know the answers?

* (0) ....*What*........ did Thomas Edison invent in 1879?

* (1) .... was the first person in space?

* (2) .... is the capital of India?

* (3) .... head is on British coins?

* (4) .... river is longer? The Nile or the Mississippi?

* (5) .... real name was Norma Jean Baker?

* (6) .... was the captain of Argentina's football team
   in the 1986 World Cup?

Answers:
0 The electric light bulb 1 Yuri Gagarin
2 New Delhi 3 The Queen's 4 The Nile
5 Marilyn Monroe's 6 Diego Maradona

74e Put the words in the correct order. Then write answers that are true for you.

0 do / in / free time / what / you / your / do?
   What do you do in your free time?   ....

1 films / of / like / you / sort / do / what?
   ....

2 you / do / kind / music / of / what / like?
   ....

3 favourite / what / your / is / book?
   ....

4 can / which / play / sports / you?
   ....

5 who / admire / do / you?
   ....

6 whose / you / do / advice / follow?
   ....

75 *What's he like?*

What's he **like**?	**What was** the restaurant **like**?

We use *What + be + subject + like* to ask somebody to describe a thing or person to us –
to tell us if somebody/something is nice, old, tall, thin, etc.:
A: **What's** he **like**?   B: *He's really nice.*
A: **What were** his friends **like**?   B: *They were very friendly.*
A: **What was** the restaurant **like**?   B: *It was very noisy.*

166378

P R A C T I C E

75a Write questions. Use *what + be + like*.

0	A:	*What's your college like?* .... (your college)	B:	It's nice.
1	A:	.... (your course)	B:	It's interesting.
2	A:	.... (your lecturers)	B:	They're good.
3	A:	.... (the facilities)	B:	They're old.
4	A:	.... (the sports centre)	B:	It isn't very good.
5	A:	.... (last term)	B:	It was hard work!
6	A:	.... (your exams)	B:	They were OK.

75b Write questions. Use *what + be + like* and the phrases in the box.

Marrakesh   the food   the markets   the people
the weather   ~~your holiday in Morocco~~   your hotel

0 A: *What was your holiday in Morocco like?* ....
   B: It was wonderful, thanks.

1 A: ....
   B: It was very hot.

2 A: ....
   B: Amazing! It's a beautiful city.

3 A: ....
   B: They were brilliant! I bought lots of things.

4 A: ....
   B: It was very nice. The rooms were beautiful.

5 A: ....
   B: It was really delicious.

6 A: ....
   B: They were very friendly.

Check 14 Questions

1 Put the words in the correct order.

1 they / gone / where / have?

....

2 she / is / time / what / coming?

....

3 laugh / he / did?

....

4 I / sit / can / here?

....

5 often / go / how / to town / you / do?

....

/ 5

2 Complete the conversation. Use the words in brackets.

A: (6) ....
camping last summer? (you / go)

B: Yes, we did. We went to France.

A: (7) .... like?
(what / the campsites / be)

B: They were brilliant! Some had really good facilities.

A: (8) .... very expensive? (they / be)

B: No, they weren't.

A: (9) .... ?
(how much / they / cost)

B: I can't remember. A few euros a night. I've got a directory of campsites that you can borrow if you like.

A: Really? Thanks!
(10) ....at it now? (I / could / look)

B: Sure. I'll get it from my room.

/ 5

3 Circle the correct answer.

11 *Which / What* one do you want?

12 *How big / How much* is your town?

13 *Which / What* colour is Mark's car?

14 *When / Where* were you on Saturday?

15 *What / How* was your hotel like?

/ 5

4 Complete the questions. Use one word in each gap.

16 A: ....'s Isabel like?

B: She's very nice.

17 A: .... do you know her?

B: I met her at a party.

18 A: .... party was it?

B: Kirsty's.

19 A: .... does she live?

B: In south London.

20 A: .... does she do?

B: She's a student.

/ 5

Total: / 20

✓ Self-check

Wrong answers	Look again at	Try CD-ROM
3, 4, 6, 8, 10	Unit 72	Exercise 72
1, 5, 9, 12, 14, 17, 19	Unit 73	Exercise 73
2, 11, 13, 18, 20	Unit 74	Exercise 74
7, 15, 16	Unit 75	Exercise 75

Now do **Check 14**

-ing forms and infinitives

76 *Dancing is fun.*

| Dancing is fun. | Swimming is good for you. | Flying a plane isn't easy. |

We can use the *-ing* form of a verb like a noun, as the subject of a sentence.

▶▶ *See Appendix 5: Spelling rules for verbs + -ing, page 170.*

PRACTICE

76a Complete the sentences. Use the correct form of the verbs in brackets.

0 ....*Skiing*............ is exciting. (ski)

1 .... is easy. (cycle)

2 .... is very good for you. (run)

3 Does .... cost a lot of money? (sail)

4 .... isn't difficult. (skate)

5 Is .... dangerous? (climb)

6 .... is cheap and fun. (camp)

76b Complete the sentences. Use the correct form of the verbs in the box. Then say if you agree or disagree. If you agree, put a tick (✓) in the box. If you disagree, put a cross (✗) in the box.

| be | do | follow | have | ~~learn~~ | ~~play~~ | shop | talk | ~~watch~~ |

0 ....*Watching*............ TV is bad for you. ☐

1 .... a foreign language is hard work. ☐

2 .... computer games is fun. ☐

3 .... for clothes is boring. ☐

4 .... sport is more interesting than watching it. ☐

5 .... about problems is useful. ☐

6 .... other people's advice isn't always a good idea. ☐

7 .... money isn't the most important thing in life. ☐

8 .... happy isn't always easy. ☐

77 I like dancing.

I **like** danc**ing**. Do you **enjoy** cycl**ing**? I **prefer** walk**ing**.

We use the -ing form of a verb after certain verbs (e.g. like, enjoy, prefer, stop):
I **like** danc**ing**. Do you **enjoy** cycl**ing**? I **prefer** walk**ing**. **Stop** laugh**ing**!

▶▶ **For a list of verbs followed by the -ing form, see Appendix 9, page 171.**

P R A C T I C E

77a Complete the sentences. Use the correct form of the verbs in brackets. For the first verb in each sentence, use the present simple.

0 My brother ....*hates doing*............ the washing-up. (hate / do)

1 He .... (prefer / cook)

2 I .... my room. (not mind / tidy)

3 My parents .... DVDs. (love / watch)

4 My sister .... late. (like / get up)

5 She .... to bed early. (not like / go)

6 We .... dinner together. (enjoy / have)

77b Complete the e-mail. Use the correct form of the verbs in the box.

get ~~have~~ meet read ~~talk~~ visit work

⊖ ⊖ ⊖   New Message   ⊂⊃

Hi, Sarah!

How are you? I had a great holiday, thanks. Mexico is a wonderful country and I can't stop (0) ....*talking*........ about it. I miss (1) .... lots of new places, but it's nice here at home, and I love (2) .... a hot shower every day!

I've just finished (3) .... my 200 (!) emails. I had one from Gemma. She's suggested (4) .... on Friday – with you and Helen. Can you come? Guess what? Helen's just got engaged! I can't imagine (5) .... married at the moment. Can you?

Have you started (6) .... on your project for next term? I haven't thought about mine yet. Anyway, that's all for now. See you on Friday.

Love,
Jenny

---

78 *I want to go home.*

| I **want to go** home. | He **promised to come.** | We **agreed to meet** him. |

We use the *to*-infinitive after certain verbs (e.g. *want, promise, agree, decide*):
I want to go home.   *He promised to come.*   *We agreed to meet* him.

▶▶   *For a list of verbs followed by the to-infinitive, see Appendix 10, page 171.*

P R A C T I C E

78a Complete the conversations. Use the correct form of the verbs in brackets.

   0 A: Why did you lend Matt your laptop?
      B: He asked ....*to borrow*........ it. He needed it for his project. (borrow)

   1 A: What time do we need .... there? (be)
      B: At about eight o'clock.

   2 A: Congratulations!
      B: Thanks! I didn't expect .... my test at all! (pass)

   3 A: Are you going now?
      B: Yes. I promised .... Laura in town at six. (meet)

   4 A: How are you getting to the station?
      B: Ben's offered .... me in his car. (take)

   5 A: Did you agree .... the party? (organise)
      B: Yes. Amir and I are going to do it.

   6 A: Have you got your photos?
      B: Oh no! I forgot .... them! (bring)

   7 A: Is Jess coming?
      B: No, she doesn't want .... tonight. (go out)

   8 A: I learned .... when I was eighteen. (drive)
      B: Have you got a car?

78b Complete the extract from a magazine article. Use the correct form of the verbs in the box.

| get   improve   live   move   ~~speak~~   ~~spend~~   stay |

Kelly Wilson is studying in Berlin. She wanted (0) ....*to spend*........ a year abroad, so she decided (1) .... there. 'It's a great experience for me,' she says. 'I'm learning (2) .... in another country. I plan (3) .... here for another six months. After my degree, I hope (4) .... a job here. I need (5) .... German very well for that, so I'm trying (6) .... my German. It isn't easy!'

79 *I'd like to play. / I like playing.*

> **I'd like to play** tennis on Saturday.   **I like playing** tennis.

- We use *would like* + *to*-infinitive to say that we want to do something. *Would like* is a polite way of saying 'I want'. The short form is *'d like*:
  I'd like to play tennis on Saturday.

- We use *Would you like* + *to*-infinitive to offer something to somebody, or to invite them to do something with us: **Would you like to stay** with us?

- *like* + *-ing* is different. Compare:
  I'd like to play tennis on Saturday. (= I want to play tennis on Saturday.)
  I like playing tennis. (= I enjoy playing tennis.)

P R A C T I C E

79a Circle the correct answer.

0 I *('d like to leave)* / *like leaving* at five. I've got football training at six.

1 Nina *would like to be* / *likes being* a doctor. She wants to go to medical school.

2 Ken *would like to work* / *likes working* here. He's worked here for ten years.

3 *Would you like to go* / *Do you like going* to the cinema with me tomorrow?

4 Tom *would like to watch* / *likes watching* the match at seven this evening.

5 They *'d like to have* / *like having* parties. They have two every year.

6 I *'d like to listen* / *like listening* to the radio. I always listen to Radio 1.

7 Where *would you like to go* / *do you like going* tonight?

8 They *'d like to live* / *like living* here. They've lived here for years.

9 *Would you like to have* / *Do you like having* dinner with us next Saturday?

10 Lisa's got lots of books. She *'d like to read* / *likes reading*.

79b Complete the conversations. Use *would like* or *like* and the correct form of the verbs in brackets.

A: I (0) .... *'d like to go* .... (go) to Turkey this summer.

　(1) ...*whould you like to come*... (you / come) with me? There are some cheap flights in June.

B: Can I tell you later? I (2) .... (visit) Philip in June if he's free. I (3) .... (stay) with him. We always have a good time together.

A: (4) ...*do you like working*... (you / work) here?

B: Yes, the people are nice and I (5) ...*like to help*... (help) the customers. But I don't earn much money, so I (6) ...*whould like to find*... (find) another job.

80 *I went there to get a book.*

> I went there **to get** a book. I often go there **to look** at their new books.

We can use the *to*-infinitive to explain why we do something:
*I went there **to get** a book.* (= I went there because I wanted to get a book.)

P R A C T I C E

80a Match and make sentences.

0	I used my new camera	b	a	to finish her History project.
1	We went to the shop	i	b	to take photos of the festival.
2	You need two keys	c	c	to open the front door.
3	He went to the airport	g	d	to invite him to the meal.
4	Aisha is staying at college late	a	e	to listen to the news.
5	We're going to the sports centre	h	f	to get some fresh air.
6	She turned on the radio	e	g	to pick up his friend.
7	I'm going to phone Matt	d	h	to play volleyball.
8	I went for a walk	f	i	to buy some ice cream.

80b Join the sentences.

0   I started doing aerobics. I wanted to get fit.
I started doing aerobics to get fit.

1   I'm going to Italy. I want to improve my Italian.
I'm going to Italy to get improve italian.

2   I've stopped using my mobile phone. I want to save money.
I stoped using my to get sve mny

3   I've left the drama group. I want to spend more time on my course.
I left the to get spend more tm on c~

4   I've joined a chat group. I want to make some new friends.
I've to want to make some

5   I'm going to Germany. I want to study Economics.
to way

6   I'm writing to some colleges. I want to ask about their courses.

7   I got a job as a waitress. I wanted to earn some extra money.

8   I'm studying Psychology. I want to understand the human mind.

Check 15 -ing forms and infinitives

1 Choose and complete the sentences.

1 (to lose, losing)
Jessica's trying ......to lose...... weight.

2 (To travel, Travelling)
...travelling...... to other countries is very exciting.

3 (to look, looking)
I'm going to town .....looking..... for some shoes.

4 (to go, going)
I'd like ....going..... to the beach tomorrow.

5 (to drive, driving)
Do you enjoy ....to driving..?

6 (to work, working)
He really misses ...working..... with Rob and Matt.

/ 6

2 Complete the message from a message board on the Internet. Use the correct form of the verbs in brackets.

My name is Rubén and I'm from Spain. I've come to London (7) ...doing..... (do) a master's degree in Plant Science. I'm enjoying (8)......being..... (be) here, but (9) ....living.... (live) in a foreign country is difficult. I don't know many people and I'd like (10) ...to make... (make) some new friends.

I love (11) ...eating.... (eat) out and I want (12) ...to try.... (try) all the different kinds of food here. I also like (13)...walking... (walk) in the countryside and I hope (14) ...to visit... (visit) some of the national parks in Britain.

/ 8

3 Complete the sentences. Use the correct form of the verbs in the box.

| buy cook do play read watch |

15 I'm saving my money ......to buy......... a computer.

16 Would you like ...to read....... this magazine?

17 I'm learning ...to play...... the guitar.

18 I've promised ...to cook.... dinner tonight.

19 ......watching... TV is very relaxing.

20 Do you like ...doing.... puzzles?

/ 6

4 Complete the sentences. Use one word in each gap.

21 Steve offered ......to...... help us.

22 I'd ......like...... to buy those shoes.

23 How long have you had this job?
......do...... you like working here?

24 Lisa and Anna went to Cambridge ......to...... visit their cousins.

25 ......do...... you like to come with us next Saturday?

/ 5

Total: / 25

That clauses

81 *I think that ..., I'm sure that ...*

> **I think that I can come** on Sunday. **I'm sure that we'll have** a good time. **I hope that Ryan brings** his football. **He says that he's got** a new one.

- We can use *that* + subject + verb after:
  - the verbs *think, believe, know, hope, say* and *tell*:
    I think that I can come. **I hope that Ryan brings** his football.
  - the adjectives *sure, certain, sorry* and *afraid*:
    I'm sure that we'll have a good time. **I'm afraid that I can't help** you.
- We can leave out *that*: **I think I can come.** **I'm sure we'll have** a good time.

 We use an object after *tell* but not after *say*. Compare:
*He **says** (that) he's got a new football.*
*He **tells me** (that) he's got a new football.*

P R A C T I C E

81a **Lisa is going on holiday tomorrow. Complete the sentences. Use the present simple of the verbs in brackets.**

0 I hope ....*(that) the weather's*.... good. (the weather / be)

1 I hope .... nice. (our hotel rooms / be)

2 I believe .... near the beach. (the hotel / be)

3 I think .... the sea from the hotel.
(we / can / see)

4 I know .... some great shops there. (there / be)

5 I hope .... good. (the food / be)

6 I hope .... her MP3 player. (Emma / bring)

7 I believe .... a camera. (Kim / have got)

8 I know .... us to the station.
(Emma's father / can / drive)

9 I believe .... our tickets. (Emma / have got)

10 I think .... on Sunday. (Becky / might / come)

81b **Complete the sentences about Anna and Tom. Use *say* or *tell* and the information in the sentences below.**

Anna's studying Art and Design. She loves her course. Her teachers are excellent. The facilities are brilliant.

Tom doesn't like his course. It's too difficult. He wants to change to Business Studies.

0 Anna ......*tells*...... me that ......*she's studying*...... Art and Design.

1 She .... that .... her course.

2 She .... me that .... excellent.

3 She .... that .... brilliant.

4 Tom .... me that .... his course.

5 He .... that .... too difficult.

6 He .... me that .... to change to Business Studies.

81c **Write sentences. Use the adjectives in brackets.**

0 I can't come to your concert on Friday. (afraid)
I'm afraid (that) I can't come to your concert on Friday.

1 You'll be fine. (sure)
....

2 Your performance will be brilliant. (certain)
....

3 I won't see you. (sorry)
....

4 I have to go to London on Friday. (afraid)
....

5 I've promised to go to my uncle's 50th birthday party. (afraid)
....

6 Your concert will be a big success. (certain)
....

7 You've practised a lot. (sure)
....

8 I'll miss it. (very sorry)
....

Relative clauses

82   *the man who lives next door*

> That's the man **who lives next door to us**. His wife's got a shop **which sells all kinds of bags**. The little dog **that's in the garden** is hers.

- A relative clause is a part of a sentence. We use relative clauses to say which person or thing we are talking about, or to give more information about it.
- We use *who* to talk about people: *That's the man **who** lives next door to us.*
- We use *which* to talk about things or animals:
  *His wife's got a shop **which** sells all kinds of bags.*
  *They've got a black cat **which** sleeps on our garage roof.*
- We use *that* to talk about people, things or animals:
  *I met a boy **that** knows your brother.*   *Where's the key **that** was on my desk?*
  *The little dog **that**'s in the garden is hers.*

 *That's the man **who lives** next door to us.*
  (Not *That's the man ~~who he lives~~ next door to us.*)
  *Where's the key **that was** on my desk?*
  (Not *Where's the key ~~that it was~~ on my desk?*)

PRACTICE

82a Circle the correct answer.

  0 The person (*who*)/*which* understands me the best is my friend Lucy.

  1 A friend *who* /*which* has got a car is going to drive us to the station.

  2 The rooms *who* /*that* have the best view of the park are those at the back.

  3 The students *who* /*which* have got exams often work late in the library.

  4 The buses *who* /*that* stop here go to the town centre.

  5 Danielle's going to stay in a hostel *who* /*which* is near the campsite.

  6 Do you know the girl *which* /*that* lives opposite my house?

  7 I've got some new trainers *who* /*which* are really nice.

  8 The letter *who* /*that* was on the table this morning is for Peter.

  9 Somebody *who* /*which* is in my group at college lent me this camera.

  10 Kelly's going to bring a cousin *who* /*which* is visiting from France.

82b **Join the sentences. Use *who* or *that*.**

0 A boy plays the drums in our band. He's only sixteen.
The boy who/that plays the drums in our band is only sixteen.

1 A girl sings in our band. She's very good.

....

2 A man teaches me the guitar. He's a very good musician.

....

3 A friend gave me her guitar. She bought a new one.

....

4 Some people came to our first gig. They enjoyed it.

....

5 Some people talked to us after the gig. They said nice things.

....

82c **Join the sentences. Use *which* or *that*.**

0 A butterfly is a kind of insect. It has large colourful wings.
A butterfly is a kind of insect which/that has large colourful wings.

1 Chalk is a kind of rock. It is soft and white.

....

2 An eagle is a big, strong bird. It eats meat.

....

3 A cactus is a plant. It grows in hot dry places.

....

4 A giraffe is an animal. It has a very long neck and long legs.

....

5 A glacier is a large quantity of ice. It moves slowly down a valley.

....

82d **Complete the sentences. Use *who, which* or *that* and the phrases in the box.**

> are in the north   crosses the river   divides the city in two
> made lots of musical instruments   ~~had a big swimming pool~~
> took us to some interesting places   lived in the ground

0 We stayed in a hotel *which/that had a big swimming pool* .

1 The hotel was near the river ....

2 We had a great tour guide ....

3 Every day we took the boat ....

4 I bought a drum from a man ....

5 I was afraid of the snakes ....

6 We visited the mountains ....

83 *the boy by the door*

> The boy **by the door** is Luke's friend. The girl **next to him** is Louise.

- We can use preposition + noun instead of a complete relative clause:
  *The boy **by the door** is Luke's friend.* (= the boy **who is standing by the door**)
- We can use prepositions of place (*above, at, behind, by,* etc.) in this way.
- And we can use these phrases in this way: *at the back/front, in the corner/middle, on the left/right, in* (*the green dress*), *with* (*red hair/glasses*).

PRACTICE

83a Re-write the sentences. Leave out part of the relative clause.

0   The man who's on the left is my uncle.
  The man on the left is my uncle.
....

1   The woman who's at the back is my grandmother.
  ....

2   The little boy who's in the middle is my brother.
  ....

3   The girl who's next to him is my cousin.
  ....

4   The man who's on the right is my dad.
  ....

5   The woman who's next to my dad is my aunt.
  ....

83b Look at the picture and complete the sentences.

0   The boy ......*in the black T-shirt is Stephen.*...... . (black T-shirt)

1   The girl .... (short dark hair)

2   The boy .... (back)

3   The boy .... (glasses)

4   The girl .... (front)

5   The girl .... (lamp)

Linking words and structures

84 and, but, or, because, so

> We went to our favourite café, **but** it was shut. I was hungry, **so** I bought some crisps.
> We sat in the park **because** it was sunny.

We use:

- *and* to link sentences that describe similar actions or situations. We do not have to repeat the subject of the first sentence after *and*:
  *We went to town **and (we)** met Ross.*

- *but* to link sentences that describe different actions or situations:
  *I asked him, **but** he didn' t answer.*

- *or* to link sentences that describe two possible actions or situations:
  *We can wait here **or** we can go to the cafeteria.*

- *because* to say that something was the reason for an action or situation. We can start a sentence with *because*. Notice when we use a comma (,):
  *We left early **because** Ben was tired.   **Because** Ben was tired, we left early.*

- *so* to say that something happened as a result of an action or situation:
  *I was hungry, **so** I bought some crisps.*

 Compare: *I bought some crisps **because** I was hungry.* (reason)
*I was hungry, **so** I bought some crisps.* (result)

PRACTICE

84a Complete the sentences. Use *and, but* or *or*.

  0 We left the car in the village ......*and*...... walked to the beach.

  1 Were there a lot of people there .... was the beach empty?

  2 It was very cold, ... we had a good time.

  3 Matt was tired, ... he came with us.

  4 Did Steven come with you too .... did he stay at home?

  5 We made a fire .... cooked some fish.

  6 I don't like fish, ... I ate some.

  7 We had some sandwiches too, ... I didn't eat any.

  8 Lucy played the guitar .... sang some songs.

  9 Did you sleep on the beach .... did you go home?

  10 Did Matt walk to the beach .... did he get a taxi?

84b **Complete the sentences. Use** *so* **or** *because.*

    o Anna's studying Biology and Chemistry ....*because*........ she wants to be a doctor.

    1 I didn't pass my exams, ... I have to take them again this year.

    2 I'm leaving in a few minutes .... I've got football practice at five.

    3 Philip isn't here today .... he's ill.

    4 I'm not enjoying my course .... it's too easy.

    5 Rachel's moving to London, ... she's having a party on Saturday.

    6 Everyone's very nice, ... I've made a lot of friends.

84c **Circle the correct answer.**

In 2005, Steve Vaught decided to change his life. He was unhappy about his body (0) *and* / *but* wanted to lose weight, (1) *so* / *because* he decided to do something about it. He walked from the west coast of the United States to the east – a journey of 4,800 kilometres!

The journey took him more than a year (2) *so* / *because* he walked slowly.

He didn't have much money, (3) *so* / *but* he stayed in cheap hotels (4) *or* / *so* he camped. He tried to eat healthy food, (5) *and* / *but* in some places he couldn't buy any fruit or vegetables.

Lots of television and radio stations followed his journey (6) *and* / *but* he often met people who knew about him. He became very popular in the US.

85 *first, next, then, after that, finally*

First we had some salad. **Next** we had some pasta. **Then** we had some chicken. **After that** we had some ice cream and **finally** we had some coffee.

● We use *first, next, then, after that* and *finally* to describe the order of actions. We use *first* for the first action and *finally* for the last action. We can use *next, then* and *after that* for the rest of the actions.

● We often use these words when we talk about the past: ***First** we had some salad. **Next** we had some pasta. **Then** we had some chicken. **After that** we had some ice cream and **finally** we had some coffee.*

● We also use them when we give instructions: ***First,** you mix the sugar, eggs and flour together. **Then,** you add the butter. **Next,** you put the mixture in two tins. **After that,** you cook it in the oven for about half an hour and **finally,** you put jam on each cake.*

● When we use these words to give instructions, we often use a comma after them. We do not usually use a comma when we use them to talk about the past.

P R A C T I C E

85a Circle the correct answer.

We did a lot yesterday in London. (0) *First* / *Next* we went shopping and bought some clothes. (1) *Finally* / *After that* we went to Buckingham Palace. (2) *Next* / *After* we had lunch in a very nice café. (3) *Then* / *First* we sat in Hyde Park for an hour or two. (4) *Next* / *After* we walked around the park and (5) *after that* / *finally* we went to the Science Museum. (6) *Then* / *Finally* we had dinner in a lovely Indian restaurant.

85b Put the sentences in the correct order. Use the pictures to help you. Then complete them with *first, next, then, after that* and *finally*.

a ☐ .... I got a bus to my friend's town. He met me at the bus station.

b ☐ .... she took us home in her car.

c 0 ......*First*........ my brother took me to the railway station on his motorbike.

d ☐ .... we arrived at their flat.

e ☐ .... I got the train to Plymouth.

f ☐ .... we walked to his mum's office.

g ☐ .... I got the boat to Santander in Spain.

85c Complete the instructions for painting a room. Use the words in the box and *first, next, then, after that* and *finally*.

| buy | ~~choose~~ | leave | measure | move | paint | put |

(0) ___First, choose___ a colour for the walls. Do you want a relaxing colour or an exciting one? Paint a large piece of paper with this colour and put it on a wall. (1) .... it there for a few days and (2) .... it on a different wall. Do you like the colour? (3) .... the walls. How big are they? (4) .... enough paint for them.
(5) .... the furniture out of the room and cover the floor.
(6) .... the walls and enjoy their new colour!

Conditional and time clauses

86 If I see her, I'll tell her.

> **If** I **see** her, I**'ll tell** her. I**'ll call** you **if** she **wants** to come.

- We use first conditional sentences to talk about something that may happen in the future, as a result of something else.
- To form first conditional sentences, we use *if* + present simple for the possible action or situation, and *will/won't* for the result.
  If I **see** her, I**'ll tell** her.   **If** they**'re** busy, I **won't ask** them.
- The *if* clause can come at the beginning of the sentence or in the middle. When it comes at the beginning, we put a comma (,) after it:
  If she wants to come, I'll call you.   *I'll call you if she wants to come.*

PRACTICE

86a Complete these first conditional sentences. Use the correct form of the verbs in brackets.

  0 If we go now, we ....*'ll get*........... a nice table. (get)

  1 If there aren't any tables inside, we .... outside. (sit)

  2 We'll get too hot if we .... in the sun. (sit)

  3 If I have a big lunch, I .... this evening. (not eat)

  4 I'll be hungry later if I .... now. (not eat)

  5 I .... Sally if I get home early. (phone)

  6 If I .... her, I'll ask her about the barbecue tomorrow. (phone)

86b Complete these first conditional sentences. Use the correct form of the verbs in brackets.

  0 If you ....*give*.......... (give) me your phone number, I ....*'ll call*.......... (call) you.

  1 I .... (stay) at home if I .... (not feel) better.

  2 If we .... (be) late, they .... (not wait) for us.

  3 If you .... (go) to the party, I .... (come) with you.

  4 She .... (be) disappointed if you .... (not be) there.

  5 What .... (you / say) if he .... (ask) you?

  6 He .... (not see) that note if you .... (leave) it there.

86c **Write first conditional sentences.**

0 you / come / by train → I / meet / you at the station
If you come by train, I'll meet you at the station.

1 the train / leave / London at twelve → it / be / here at two

....

2 Lucy / call / me → I / ask / her to come with us

....

3 you / not want / to play tennis → we / do / something else

....

4 you / need / a tennis racket → I / lend / you mine

....

5 my brother / not be / busy → he / play / with us

....

6 my dad / finish / work early → he / drive / us to the sports centre

....

7 it / rain → we / stay / at home

....

8 you / be / interested → I / show / you my paintings

....

9 you / like / my paintings → I / draw / a picture of you

....

10 Matt / let / us use his computer → we / visit / Jo's new website

....

86d **Complete these first conditional sentences. Use the correct form of the verbs in brackets.**

TIPS FOR MANAGING YOUR WORK

➲ If you (0) ....*organise*.......... (organise) your things carefully, you
(1) .... (find) them quickly.

➲ If you (2) .... (make) a list of the things that you have to do,
you (3) .... (not forget) to do them.

➲ If you (4) .... (not take) regular breaks, you
(5) .... (feel) tired and you (6) .... (not work)
well.

➲ If you (7) .... (divide) a difficult task into smaller tasks, you
(8) .... (do) it more easily.

➲ If you (9) .... (plan) your work, you (10) ....
(not worry) about it.

87 *I'll tell her when I see her.*

> I'll tell her **when** I **see** her.   I'll give you my address **before** I **leave**.

- We can use *when* and *before* to talk about the future.
- We use the present simple (not *will*) after *when* and *before*:
  *I'll tell her **when** I **see** her.* (Not *I'll tell her **when** I'll see her.*)
- The clause with *when* or *before* can come at the beginning of the sentence or in the middle. When it comes at the beginning, we put a comma (,) after it:
  When I see her, I'll tell her.   I'll tell her when I see her.

P R A C T I C E

87a Complete the sentences. Use the correct form of the verbs in brackets.

o When Sophie .... *moves* .... to Spain, she won't take her cat with her. (move)

1 They'll stay with us for a few days before they .... London. (leave)

2 .... us when you arrive? (you / call)

3 We .... back before Jack gets here. (be)

4 When I .... him, I'll give him your message. (see)

5 No, I won't be late. I'll be there before the lesson .... (start)

6 He .... very pleased when he sees these photos. (be)

7 Before I .... the form, I'll ask Jo to have a look at it. (sign)

8 I .... to him when he comes back. (talk)

87b Circle the correct answer.

o When (*I get*)/*I'll get* back, *I show* /(*I'll show*) you my new books.

1 *I make* /*I'll make* some food before *they arrive* /*they'll arrive*.

2 Before *I buy* /*I'll buy* this computer, *I ask* /*I'll ask* Tom for some advice.

3 What *does he do* /*will he do* when *he leaves* /*he'll leave* college?

4 *Do you have* /*Will you have* a holiday before *you start* /*you'll start* your course?

5 *I decide* /*I'll decide* when *I know* /*I'll know* more about it.

6 *I have* /*I'll have* a shower before *I go* /*I'll go* out.

7 When *I go* /*I'll go* to the supermarket, *I get* /*I'll get* some milk.

8 *He calls* /*He'll call* us when *he gets* /*he'll get* our message.

9 *We visit* /*We'll visit* them before *we leave* /*we'll leave*.

10 *I call* /*I'll call* you when *I get* /*I'll get* your e-mail.

Check 16 Clauses

1 Complete the sentences. Use the correct form of the verbs in brackets.

1 We'll phone them when we .... to the campsite. (get)

2 We'll put our tent up before we .... them. (meet)

3 If we get there late, we .... them on Sunday. (see)

4 If they're tired, we .... much. We can just talk. (not do)

5 They'll laugh when they .... about our trip last weekend! (hear)

6 If Emma wants a game of tennis, John .... with her. (play)

7 If he doesn't play with her, she .... very disappointed. (be)

/ 7

2 Circle the correct answer.

I had a nice day yesterday. I got up late (8) *and / but* went into town. I met some friends (9) *who / which* go to college with me. We went to a café (10) *who / which* has really good coffee! I was hungry, (11) *so / because* I had a sandwich, too. Next we went shopping and (12) *after that / finally* we had an ice cream in the park. Then we saw a film (13) *who / that* was very good – I really liked the music. Kirsty (14) *says / tells* that there's a CD of it. (15) *First / Finally* we came home on the bus.

/ 8

3 Complete the sentences. Use one word in each gap.

16 First we went to the museum. .... we sat in the park for half an hour.

17 The girl .... the blue T-shirt and jeans lives in my street.

18 I hope .... you do well in your exams tomorrow.

19 Do you want to get the bus .... would you like to walk home?

20 The little boy .... the left is my nephew.

21 I'm afraid .... I can't help you. I'm really sorry.

22 I .... tell Sarah about the party when I see her.

23 The man .... answered the phone was Jack's father.

24 I wanted to go out, ... I couldn't. I was too tired.

25 The painting .... is hanging on that wall cost him £50,000.

/ 10

Total: / 25

✓ Self-check

Wrong answers	Look again at	Try CD-ROM
14, 18, 21	**Unit 81**	Exercise 81
9, 10, 13, 23, 25	**Unit 82**	Exercise 82
17, 20	**Unit 83**	Exercise 83
8, 11, 19, 24	**Unit 84**	Exercise 84
12, 15, 16	**Unit 85**	Exercise 85
3, 4, 6, 7	**Unit 86**	Exercise 86
1, 2, 5, 22	**Unit 87**	Exercise 87

Now do **Check 16**

Prepositions and phrasal verbs

88   *at the door, in the kitchen, on the table*

Ben's **at** the door.   Kim's **in** the kitchen.   There's a letter for you **on** the table.

We use *at, in* and *on* to say where something or somebody is.

at the door

at the table

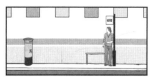
at the bus stop

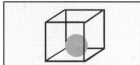
in the box
in the kitchen

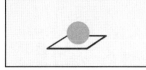
in the garden
in a town

on the table
on the floor

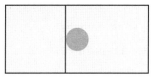
on the wall
on the door

▶▶   *For more prepositions of place, see Unit 89.*

P R A C T I C E

88a Circle the correct answer.

0   We're going to have our lunch *on* /*in* the park.

1   Why are you lying *on* /*in* the floor?

2   Kirsty's going to meet us *at*/*on* the station at five.

3   There's a message for you *on* /*in* the fridge door.

4   I put my notes *at* /*in* my file, but now I can't find them.

5   There are some knives and forks *at* /*in* that drawer.

6   Tom's playing tennis *on* /*at* the sports centre.

7   Do you like swimming *at* /*in* the sea?

8   Your sunglasses are *on* /*at* that chair.

88b **Look at the picture and complete the sentences. Use *at, in* or *on* and the words in brackets.**

0 There's a big bowl ......*on the table*... . (table)

1 There are some oranges .... (bowl)

2 There are a few pictures .... (wall)

3 Jessica's sitting .... (table)

4 Her bag's .... (chair)

5 Her books are .... (bag)

6 Ben's standing .... (window)

7 Jessica and Ben are .... (kitchen)

8 There's a vase of flowers .... (table)

88c **Complete the conversation. Use *at, in* or *on*.**

A: Laura's just phoned. She and Kirsty are (0) ......*at*...... the station.

B: OK. What time are we meeting them (1) .... the cinema?

A: Nine.

B: Are we going to the cinema (2) .... the town centre?

A: Yes. Are you ready?

B: No. I must get my watch. It's (3) .... the bathroom. And where are my keys? They were (4) .... my pocket.

A: There are some (5) .... this shelf.

B: Oh, thanks! And can you see the tickets anywhere?

A: There are some (6) .... the kitchen table. Are they the ones for the cinema?

B: Yes, great! OK, let's go!

89 *in front of the lamp, next to the phone*

We also use these prepositions to say where somebody or something is:

The photo's **in front of** the lamp.
The lamp's **behind** the photo.
The phone's **near** the photo.
The pen and paper are **next to** the phone.

The ball's **under** the desk.
The shelf's **above** the desk.
The CD player's **between** the vase and the CDs.

There's a small house **among** the trees.
It's **opposite** the bus stop.

▶▶ **For more prepositions of place, see Unit 88.**

PRACTICE

89a Look at the picture and circle the correct answer.

0 The door is (between)/behind two windows.

1 A light is *in front of /above* the door.

2 A pot of flowers is *next to /opposite* the door.

3 A bike is *opposite /under* a window.

4 A cat is *behind /in front of* the bike.

5 A car is *among /near* the house.

6 A tree is *behind /under* the house.

89b **Look at the pictures and complete the sentences. Use the prepositions in the box.**

above among behind between near next to (x2) opposite ~~under~~

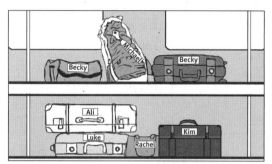

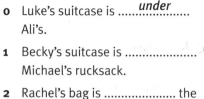
0 Luke's suitcase is .... *under* .... Ali's.

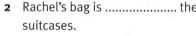
1 Becky's suitcase is .... Michael's rucksack.

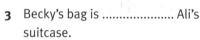
2 Rachel's bag is .... the suitcases.

3 Becky's bag is .... Ali's suitcase.

4 Michael is .... Kim.

5 Rachel is .... Luke and Kim.

6 Becky is .... Kim.

7 Kim is .... Rachel.

8 Ali is .... Michael.

89c **Look at the pictures and complete the sentences. Use the correct prepositions.**

0 There's a chemist's .... *next to* .... the café.

1 There's a bus stop .... the chemist's.

2 There's a tree .... the café.

3 There's a bin .... the tree.

4 There's a television .... the bookcase and the armchair.

5 There's a guitar .... the armchair.

6 There's a mirror .... the armchair.

7 There's a DVD player .... the television.

8 There's a teddy bear .... the books.

90 *from the bus stop to the cinema*

I walked **from** the bus stop **to** the cinema. I ran **across** the road.

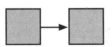

I walked **from** *the bus stop* **to** *the cinema.*

I ran **across** *the road.*

We walked **up** *the hill.*

We ran **down** *the stairs.*

We went **into** *the house.*

We came **out of** *the theatre.*

The cat jumped **onto** *the shelf.*

The vase fell **off** *the shelf.*

PRACTICE

90a Look at the pictures and circle the correct answer.

The cat walked (0) *out of* / *off* the door and climbed (1) *up* / *off* the fence. Then she jumped (2) *into* / *onto* the roof of our garage. She walked (3) *to* / *across* the roof and then she jumped (4) *down* / *into* a tree. She came (5) *down* / *up* the tree a little way and then she jumped (6) *down* / *to* the ground.

90b **Look at the pictures and complete the sentences. Use the correct prepositions and the nouns in the box.**

| the beach | the boat | the bridge | the cinema | the hill | ~~the stairs~~ |

 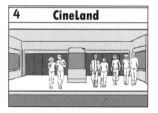 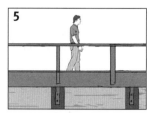

0 She walked .....*up the stairs*..... .

1 They walked here ....

2 He cycled ....

3 We drove ....

4 Everyone came .... at ten.

5 He walked ....

90c **Complete the sentences. Use the prepositions in the box.**

| down | from | ~~into~~ | off | onto | out of | to |

0 Lucy came ....*into*........ the room and sat down on a chair at the back.

1 We skiied fast .... the mountain.

2 All my clothes fell .... my bag when I picked it up.

3 We went .... the sports centre and played volleyball.

4 Some oranges fell .... the tree and landed on the ground.

5 The boys climbed .... a big rock and sat on it.

6 How far is it .... the station to your house?

90d **Complete the extract from a letter. Use the correct prepositions.**

I met Philip at his house and we cycled (0) .....*from*.... there (1) .....*to*......
the swimming pool. The pool is on the other side of town, so we had to
cycle (2) ...*across*...town. There is a big hill on the way there. We cycled
up it slowly, and then came (3) ....*down*... quickly. At the bottom of the
hill, I fell (4) ....*off*.. my bike! I hurt my arm, but I was all right. We
were very hot when we got to the pool, so we jumped (5) ...*into*.... the water
immediately. We stayed in the pool for about an hour. When I came
(6) ...*out of*.... the water, I felt wonderful – very cool and relaxed.

91 *on Monday, in the morning, at one o'clock*

> We went to London **on** Monday. We went shopping **in** the morning. We had lunch **at** one o'clock.

- We use *on* with days and dates: ***on** Monday(s)*   ***on** Friday*   ***on** 3rd July*
- We use *in* with parts of the day and longer periods of time: months, seasons, years and centuries:
  ***in** the morning*   ***in** June*   ***in** the winter*   ***in** 2007*   ***in** the 19th century*
- We use *at* with clock times: ***at** two o' clock*   ***at** midday*   ***at** dinnertime*
  We also say: ***at** night, **at** the weekend, **at** Christmas, **at** Easter, **at** the moment*
- We do not use *at, in* or *on* when we use *next, last, every, this, yesterday* or *tomorrow*: *next weekend*   *last Monday*   *this winter*   *tomorrow morning*

⚠️ **on** *Friday*   **in** *the evening*   **on** *Friday evening*

PRACTICE

91a **Write the words and phrases in the box in the correct group.**

> ~~1999~~   14th April   August   Easter   half past three   my birthday   noon
> Saturday   the evening   the moment   the summer   Thursday morning

on	in	at
✓14th April	1999	at Easter ✓
on August	in Auges	at half past three ✓
on my Mrn	...	at birthday
on Satur	... summer	moment
✓		at noon

91b **Circle the correct answer.**

New Message

(0) **On** / In Saturday, I went to help at a nature reserve. I got up
(1) *in / at* half past seven and after breakfast I cycled to the reserve.
I was wearing lots of warm clothes – it's cold here (2) *in / at* the
spring. At the reserve, the organiser gave me and the other helpers
our tasks for the day. (3) *On / In* the morning, I helped to repair
a path and (4) *on / in* the afternoon, I worked on a picnic area for
visitors. (5) *In / At* lunchtime, we sat and talked. It was nice to meet
the other helpers. I'm going back there (6) *on / in* 15th June – and
next year I'm going to go to a reserve in Scotland.

91c **Complete the sentences. Use *at, in* or *on*. If a sentence does not need a preposition, write – on the line.**

0 Jack had a great party ....–........ last weekend.

1 He had a good one .... June, too.

2 He has a party .... every year.

3 I might have one .... Christmas.

4 Are you going to college .... tomorrow?

5 We've got tests every day .... this week.

6 And I've got an exam .... Thursday.

91d **Complete the sentences. Use *at, in* or *on*. Then look at Mark's notes and say if the sentences are right or wrong. If a sentence is right, put a tick (✓) in the box. If it is wrong, put a cross (✗) in the box.**

> **Saturday and Sunday:** working in DVD shop
>
> **Monday:** driving test – 12.30
>
> **Tuesday:** meet Lucy
>
> **Wednesday:** take Mum's car to garage – 8.30 am
>
> **Thursday:** Craig here – lunchtime; collect car – afternoon
>
> **Friday:** gig with Richard; meet at station – 9.00 pm

0 He's working in the DVD shop ....*at*........ the weekend. ☑

1 He's taking his driving test .... half past ten .... Monday. ☐

2 He's meeting Lucy .... Friday. ☐

3 He's taking his mum's car to the garage .... Tuesday morning. ☐

4 His friend Craig is coming to his house .... lunchtime on Thursday. Then, ... the afternoon, he has to collect his mum's car from the garage. ☐

5 .... Friday evening, he's going to a gig with his friend Richard. He's meeting him at the station .... 9.00 pm. ☐

91e **Write answers that are true for you. Use *at, in* or *on* if you need them.**

0 When were you born?   *In 1989.* ....

1 When's your birthday?   ....

2 What time do you usually get up?   ....

3 When do you usually phone your friends? ....

4 When do you usually visit your relatives? ....

5 When are you going to have a holiday? ....

92 *before the exam, during the play, after lunch*

I was nervous **before** the exam.   I felt all right **during** the exam.
I felt tired **after** the exam.

We use *before, during* and *after* (+ article) + noun to say when something happens:
*I'll be back **before** noon.*   *He fell asleep **during** the play.*   *I'll call you **after** lunch.*

 We use *for* (not *during*) for periods of time:
*We were there **for** a month.* (NOT *We were there **during** a month*.)

PRACTICE

92a Complete the sentences. Use *before, during* or *after*.

o Let's meet at Tim's house ....*before*........ the play. His mother can drive us to the theatre.

1 There's a meal .... the wedding. The wedding's at three and the meal's at five.

2 He broke his hand .... the match. Another player fell on him.

3 I have to finish my project .... the end of the term because we're getting another one next term.

4 .... a long discussion, we finally came to a decision.

5 I've got lectures all morning, so I can't phone you .... lunch.

6 They asked me some difficult questions .... the interview.

7 Mark and Amanda felt tired .... their long journey, so they went straight to bed.

8 Did you visit the Eiffel Tower .... your stay in Paris?

92b Circle the correct answer.

Rebecca suddenly became ill (o) *during* / *for* a camping trip in the summer holidays. She was ill (1) *during* / *for* a long time. A lot of people visited her (2) *during* / *for* the holidays, but then term started and everybody was very busy.

She came back to college (3) *during* / *for* a few days before Christmas and then, (4) *during* / *for* the Christmas holidays, she stayed with some relatives in France (5) *during* / *for* a week.

She's back at college now, but she sleeps (6) *during* / *for* twelve hours a night, and she sometimes gets tired (7) *during* / *for* the day. 'I want to go to sleep (8) *during* / *for* some lectures,' she told me. 'Don't worry!' I said. 'We all want to do that!'

Check 17 Prepositions of place, movement and time

1 Choose and complete the sentences.

1 (on, in)

Have you got an exam .... Wednesday?

2 (onto, into)

The cat jumped .... the wall.

3 (at, in)

Leanne and Jodie are .... the garden.

4 (from, out of)

He walked .... the room because he was angry.

5 (during, in)

I didn't feel well .... the journey.

/ 5

2 Look at the picture and complete the sentences. Use the correct prepositions.

6 The computer is .... the desk.

7 The cup is .... the computer.

8 The books are .... the computer.

9 The box of tissues is .... the books and the photo.

10 The phone is .... the photo.

/ 5

3 Complete the sentences. Use the prepositions in the box.

at before in off on

11 There aren't any pictures .... the walls.

12 Emma and her friends are .... that table in the corner.

13 Your bag might fall .... that shelf if you leave it like that.

14 I usually have a shower .... the morning.

15 I'd like to eat something .... the film.

/ 5

4 Complete what Matt says. Use a preposition in each gap. If a sentence does not need a preposition, write – on the line.

I spent the day in London with Kim yesterday. We met (16) .... ten o'clock. We went shopping and then we had lunch (17) .... a café. (18) .... lunch, we went (19) .... the Science Museum. We had a great time there. We want to go again (20) .... next week.

/ 5

Total: / 20

✓ Self-check

Wrong answers	Look again at	Try CD-ROM
3, 6, 11, 12, 17	**Unit 88**	Exercise 88
7, 8, 9, 10	**Unit 89**	Exercise 89
2, 4, 13, 19	**Unit 90**	Exercise 90
1, 14, 16, 20	**Unit 91**	Exercise 91
5, 15, 18	**Unit 92**	Exercise 92

93 *at home, in bed*

> Laura's **at home**. She's **in bed**. She hasn't got up yet because she's **on holiday**.
> Are you going to town **by bus**?

We often use *at, in, on* and *by* with nouns, without an article. We say:

- *at home, at school, at work, at college, at university*
- *in bed, in hospital, in prison, in Britain/London,* etc.
- *on holiday, on television/TV, on foot*
- *by bus, by car, by train, by plane, by boat, by bike, by road, by sea, by air*

PRACTICE

93a Circle the correct answer.

0   I've left my phone *at*/*in* home.

1   He was *at* /*in* prison for six months.

2   Did you come here *by* /*on* foot?

3   How long have you been *at* /*in* Rome?

4   I love travelling *by* /*on* plane.

5   Were you happy *at* /*in* school?

6   They're *in* /*on* holiday this week.

7   We sent our things to Australia *by* /*in* sea.

8   He's working *at* /*in* Russia this year.

9   Have you ever been *in* /*on* television?

10 Jo's got the car, so I have to go *by* /*in* bus.

93b Complete the sentences. Use *at, in, on* or *by*.

0   I stayed .....*at*...... home yesterday.

1   I stayed .... bed until 11.00!

2   There were some good programmes .... TV.

3   Mum was .... work.

4   Dad was .... Manchester.

5   He went there .... train.

6   The journey takes a long time .... road.

7   Danielle was .... college.

8   Rob was .... school.

9   My grandmother's been .... hospital since last week.

10 Matt wasn't here either. He's been .... holiday in Spain since Thursday.

93c **Complete the conversation. Use** *at, in, on* **or** *by* **and the words in the box.**

air   bed   boat   France   ~~holiday~~   school   university

A: Is your sister here with you?

B: No, she's (0) ....*on holiday*............. at the moment. She and her friend Rachel have gone camping.

A: Where have they gone?

B: Somewhere (1) ....

A: Did they fly there?

B: Yes. It's very quick when you go (2) ....

A: Yes, it is. We usually go (3) .... because we take the car. And how are your brothers?

B: Neil's fine, thanks. He's (4) .... He's studying Chemistry. And Martin's in his last year (5) .... He's not well today, so he's (6) ....

94 *interested in, good at*

Becky's **interested in** art. She's **good at** drawing.

- We use a preposition after some adjectives: *interested **in**   good **at***
- Many of these adjectives describe feelings: *afraid of, angry with, excited about, fed up with, pleased with, proud of, ready for, tired of, worried about*
- We use *good/brilliant/bad/terrible at* to talk about ability:
  *Becky's **good at** drawing.   I'm **bad at** sport.*
  *Tom's **brilliant at** Maths but he's **terrible at** History.*
- Other examples are: *different from, famous for, full of, married to*
- We use a noun, a pronoun or the *-ing* form of the verb after the preposition:
  *I'm bad at **sport**.   He's angry with **her**.   She's good at **drawing**.*

▶▶ *For a list of adjectives followed by prepositions, see Appendix 13, page 173.*

P R A C T I C E

94a Match and make sentences.

0	I'm worried	c	**a**	in some subjects.
1	I'm not ready	☐	**b**	with revising.
2	My parents may not be pleased	☐	**c**	about my exams.
3	The Maths exam will be full	☐	**d**	of difficult questions.
4	I'm bad	☐	**e**	for them.
5	I'm not interested	☐	**f**	with my results.
6	Everyone's fed up	☐	**g**	at remembering things.

94b Circle the correct answer.

0   Adam's really good *at*/*in* playing the piano.

1   His parents are very proud *for* /*of* him.

2   I'm not surprised *for* /*by* his success.

3   Does he ever get tired *of* /*from* practising?

4   He has to be careful *with* /*from* his hands.

5   He's really nervous *for* /*about* his concert next week.

6   Emma, his sister, is interested *at* /*in* music, too.

7   She's brilliant *at* /*to* playing the guitar!

8   Her concert's next month and she's very excited *about* /*of* it.

9   Their uncle's married *with* /*to* a famous musician.

10 She's very nice *with* /*to* Adam and Emma.

94c Complete the conversation. Use the correct prepositions.

A: What's Natalie like?

B: She's nice. She's very friendly and she's always very kind (0) ....*to*.......... people.

A: Is she in the basketball team with you?

B: Yes. She's very good. She's much better (1) .... basketball than me.

A: So, when's your next big match?

B: Friday. We're really excited (2) .... it, but the training session on Thursday didn't go well. The coach is usually very nice (3) .... us, but he got really angry (4) .... some of us on Friday. He wasn't pleased (5) .... us at all!

A: What are the other team like?

B: They're good, but we're not frightened (6) .... them. We're good, too!

95 *get on, sit down, look out*

> I **got on** the bus and I **sat down**.   **Look out**! There's a car coming!

- Many English verbs have two parts: a verb and a preposition or an adverb. For example: *get on, sit down, look out*.
- Sometimes the meaning of the verb does not change when we add the preposition or adverb (e.g. *sit down* = 'sit' + 'down').
- But sometimes the verb has a different meaning. (e.g. *look out* = 'be careful').
- When another verb comes after the preposition or adverb, we use the *-ing* form of this verb: *He **went on reading** his book.*

▶▶ **For a list of some common phrasal verbs, see Appendix 14, page 173.**

PRACTICE

95a Circle the correct answer.

0   Do you want to go *in* /*out* tonight? What about going to the cinema?

1   Do we get *on* /*off* the bus at the post office? Is the cinema near there?

2   I'm looking *for* /*at* my bag. I can't find it.

3   Have you looked *at* /*out* this magazine?

4   I don't want to stay *in* /*out* this evening. Let's go to the theatre.

5   I'm coming! I'm just putting *on* /*off* my boots.

6   You look tired. Why don't you lie *up* /*down* for a few minutes?

7   Buy, Anna. Come *back* /*in* and see us soon!

8   It was hot, so I took *on* /*off* my jacket.

95b Complete the extract from an e-mail. Use the phrasal verbs in the box.

> broke down   came round   gave up   ~~got up~~   rang up   set off   went on

```
● ○ ●                        New Message                        ▭

Yesterday Laura and I (0) ........got up.......... at seven and we
(1) ........................ at nine. The car was making a strange noise, but
we (2) ........................ driving. After about an hour, the car
(3) ........................ . The engine just died. We tried to find the
cause of the problem, but we (4) ........................ after twenty
minutes. I (5) ........................ the repair service and a man came
after about an hour. Luckily, the problem wasn't serious, so he fixed
it for us and we continued our journey.

We arrived in York at seven and had dinner with Katie. Later, some
friends (6) ........................ and we had a great evening together.
```

Check 18 Prepositions and phrasal verbs

1 **Choose and complete the sentences.**

1 (on, in)
My favourite film's .... TV tonight.

2 (out, at)
Look .... ! There's some glass on the floor!

3 (at, in)
Have you ever been .... hospital?

4 (for, with)
Emma isn't careful .... her things.

5 (out, over)
I went .... with my friends last night and had a great time.

6 (to, of)
We left because we were tired .... waiting to talk to somebody.

/ 6

2 **Complete the conversations. Use the prepositions in the box.**

| at for of on up with |

7 A: Are you looking .... something?
B: Yes. The biscuits. I can't find them.

8 A: Is Rachel here?
B: No. She's staying .... home today.

9 A: Are you pleased .... your exam results?
B: Yes, I am.

10 A: Do you always wake .... early?
B: No, only sometimes.

11 A: Did you cycle to the beach?
B: No. We went .... foot.

12 A: Do you like flying?
B: No. I'm afraid .... it.

/ 6

3 **Complete the extract from a letter. Use one word in each gap.**

Last week I was (13) .... holiday (14) .... Ireland with some friends. On Saturday, we went for a walk. We set (15) .... at ten and we carried (16) .... walking for two or three hours. Tom's good (17) .... reading maps, so he showed us the way. Becky's interested (18) .... plants, so she told us the names of some flowers. At one o'clock, we sat (19) .... under some trees and had some sandwiches, and then we came home (20) .... bus.

/ 8

Total: / 20

✓ **Self-check**

Wrong answers	Look again at	Try CD-ROM
1, 3, 8, 11, 13, 14, 20	**Unit 93**	Exercise 93
4, 6, 9, 12, 17, 18	**Unit 94**	Exercise 94
2, 5, 7, 10, 15, 16, 19	**Unit 95**	Exercise 95

Now do **Check 18**

Word formation

96 *interested, interesting*

Compare adjectives that end in *-ed* and adjectives that end in *-ing*:

	-ed adjective			*-ing* adjective
I'm	interest**ed**	in history.	**History** is	interest**ing**.
The students are	bor**ed**.		**Science** is	bor**ing**.

- We use *-ed* adjectives to describe how we feel.
- We use *-ing* adjectives to describe the person or thing that makes us feel that way.

PRACTICE

96a Circle the correct answer.

0 That film was very *frightened* / *frightening*.

1 I'm *tired* / *tiring*. I'm going to bed.

2 That's an *amazed* / *amazing* story!

3 I'm *bored* / *boring*. I want to go home.

4 Hi Rob! I'm *surprised* / *surprising* to see you here!

5 This music's very *relaxed* / *relaxing*.

6 Are you *excited* / *exciting* about your skiing trip?

96b Complete the messages from a message board on the Internet. Use the words in the box. You do not need all of them.

amazed   amazing   ~~bored~~   boring   excited   exciting   frightened
frightening   interested   interesting   relaxed   relaxing

Amanda344:	There's nothing to do here! I'm really (0) .....*bored*..... ! What do you do?
Jade610:	I go running for half an hour every day. It's (1) .... , but I feel good after it.
dark_eyes:	I'm (2) .... in fashion, so I make a lot of clothes.
water_baby:	I love swimming. I forget everything and I feel very (3) ....
Amanda344:	Next week I'm going on a sailing trip with the school. But I don't like the sea. It's dangerous and (4) .... I can swim, but I don't want to go.
water_baby:	Don't worry. Sailing's great. It's (5) .... because the boat moves fast.
Jade610:	Yeah. I go sailing every year and I always have a(n) (6) .... time! It's brilliant! You'll be fine.

97   *dirty, comfortable, careful*

The car's **dirty**.   These trainers are **comfortable**.   Be **careful**!

- A suffix is a letter or group of letters that we add to the end of a word to form a new word. We can form some adjectives by adding a suffix to a noun or verb.
- We can add:
  - -y: dirt → dirt**y**   smoke → smok**y**   fog → fogg**y**
  - -able: comfort → comfort**able**   fashion → fashion**able**
  - -ful: care → care**ful**   beauty → beauti**ful**   use → use**ful**

▶▶ **See Appendix 7: Spelling rules for adjectives ending -y, page 170.**

P R A C T I C E

97a **Make adjectives from the words in the table. Use -y, -able or -ful.**

-y		-able		-ful	
health	*healthy*	fashion		success	
cloud		count		pain	
noise		enjoy		colour	
fun		wash		help	
salt		accept		wonder	
dust		value		hope	

97b **Make adjectives from the words in brackets to complete the sentences. Use -y, -able or -ful.**

0   My clothes are ....*dirty*............ because I couldn't wash them on the trip. (dirt)

1   We had a great time! The trip was really .... (enjoy)

2   The weather was perfect. It was warm and .... (sun)

3   There was a .... river near the campsite. (beauty)

4   I slept well. My sleeping bag and mat were very .... (comfort)

5   Your knife was very .... , thanks. (use)

6   Fire's dangerous, of course, so we were very .... with ours. (care)

7   We climbed a mountain. The path was very .... , but it wasn't difficult. (stone)

8   Adam and Kirsty have just gone to bed. They felt tired and .... after the trip. (sleep)

98 *uncomfortable, impossible*

> I couldn't sleep at the hostel because the bed was **uncomfortable**.
> It was **impossible** to get another bed because the hostel was full.

A prefix is a group of letters that we add to the beginning of a word to form a new word. We can make some adjectives negative by adding the prefixes *un-* and *im-*:
uncomfortable (= not comfortable)   **im**possible (= not possible)

P R A C T I C E

98a Complete the sentences. Use adjectives that begin with *un-* or *im-* .

0 Something which is not important is ....*unimportant*............ .

1 Somebody who is not kind is ....

2 Something which is not possible is ....

3 Something which is not necessary is ....

4 Somebody who is not polite is ....

5 Something which is not perfect is ....

6 Something which is not usual is ....

98b Make adjectives from the words in brackets to complete the sentences. Use *un-* or *im-* .

0 Scott looked very ....*unhappy*............ . (happy)

1 I don't like our neighbours because they're .... (friendly)

2 Lisa's always very .... (patient)

3 My glasses are old and .... (fashionable)

4 He's .... because he says horrible things to people. (popular)

5 The music was very loud, so conversation was .... (possible)

6 Our band was .... because we never practised. (successful)

98c Write true sentences about people you know. Use adjectives that begin with *un-* or *im-* .

0 *My brother's always very impatient.* ....

1 ....

2 ....

3 ....

4 ....

5 ....

99 *a flower shop, a sports centre*

There's a **flower shop** near the **sports centre**.

- Some nouns have two parts: a noun + a noun. We call these nouns compound nouns. The first noun usually gives us information about the second noun: *flower shop* (= a shop that sells flowers)
- We write some of these nouns as two words: *flower shop*   *telephone call*
- And we write some of them as one word: *girlfriend*   *wheelchair*

P R A C T I C E

99a Write the compound nouns next to the sentences. Use one word from each box each time. Write all the nouns as two words.

bus	car	clothes	computer	mountain	~~post~~	tennis

ball	bike	game	~~office~~	park	shop	stop

0 You can buy stamps and post letters here.   ....*post office*..................

1 You can get on or off a bus here.   ....

2 You can buy T-shirts and jeans here.   ....

3 You play tennis with this.   ....

4 You can go up and down hills on this.   ....

5 You can leave your car here.   ....

6 You can play this with a friend.   ....

99b Complete the compound nouns. Use the words in the box. Write all the nouns as one word.

~~bag~~	bike	board	book	brush	glasses	pack	paper	suit

A: What's in your (0) hand...*bag*.............. ?
B: My (1) sun.................... , my money, a (2) hair.................... and a (3) note.................... .

A: Have you bought a (4) motor.................... yet?
B: No. I looked in the (5) news.................... yesterday, but I didn't see a cheap one.
A: There's an advert for one on the (6) notice.................... near the gym.
B: Really? Thanks. I'll look at it tomorrow.

A: Is this your (7) back.................... ?
B: Yes. I mustn't forget it! My trainers and my (8) track.................... are in it. I'm going running later.

Check 19 Word formation

1 Complete the sentences. Use the words in brackets and a prefix or suffix from the box.

-able -ful im- un- -y

1 This guidebook's very .... It has lots of information. (use)

2 Wait! Don't be so .... ! (patient)

3 The trip was very .... (enjoy)

4 Could you put all the .... cups in the sink, please? (dirt)

5 He's often rude and .... to her. (kind)

/ 5

2 Circle the correct answer.

6 We were *frightened / frightening* by the horses because they were very big.

7 When I told her the news, she was very *surprised / surprising*.

8 Your stories are *amazed / amazing*! You have some brilliant ideas.

9 I didn't feel *relaxed / relaxing*, so I couldn't sleep.

10 I was *bored / boring* because my friends weren't with me.

/ 5

3 Complete the conversation. Use compound nouns. Use one word from each box each time. Write all the nouns as two words.

Art bus Internet music sports

café centre project shop stop

Liz: Hi, Zoe. Where are you ?

Zoe: I'm at the (11) .... on Parker Street. I'm checking my e-mails. Where are you?

Liz: I'm at home. I'm drawing something for my (12) .... How about a game of tennis at the (13) .... this afternoon?

Zoe: Great idea! Shall we go by bus?

Liz: Sure. Let's meet at the (14) .... in front of the (15) .... – the one with the guitars in the window. At four o'clock?

Zoe: Fine. See you later!

/ 5

4 Make adjectives from the words in brackets to complete the extract from a letter. Use prefixes or suffixes.

My hotel room was very nice. The bed was (16) .... (comfort) and the view from the window was (17) .... (beauty). I could see the lake and the mountains. There were a lot of birds by the lake, and I saw some very (18) .... (usual) blue ones.

The weather was all right. It was (19) .... (cloud), but it didn't rain. The water in the lake was very cold, so swimming was (20) .... (possible)!

/ 5

Total: / 20

✓ **Self-check**

Wrong answers	Look again at	Try CD-ROM
6, 7, 8, 9, 10	**Unit 96**	Exercise 96
1, 3, 4, 16, 17, 19	**Unit 97**	Exercise 97
2, 5, 18, 20	**Unit 98**	Exercise 98
11, 12, 13, 14, 15	**Unit 99**	Exercise 99

Now do **Check 19**

Appendices

1 Spelling rules for plural nouns

Noun	Rule	Examples
most nouns	add -s	book → books room → rooms
nouns ending in consonant + -y	change -y to -i	baby → babies story → stories
nouns ending in vowel + -y	add -s	boy → boys day → days
nouns ending in -ch, -sh, -ss, -s or -x	add -es	match → matches brush → brushes dress → dresses box → boxes
nouns ending in -o	add -s or -es	video → videos photo → photos potato → potatoes tomato → tomatoes
nouns ending in -f or -fe	change -f to -v	shelf → shelves knife → knives

2 Spelling rules for comparative and superlative adjectives

Adjective	Rule	Examples
most adjectives	add -er or -est	old → older → oldest short → shorter → shortest
adjectives ending in -e	add -er or -est	nice → nicer → nicest safe → safer → safest
adjectives ending in -y	change -y to -i	easy → easier → easiest happy → happier → happiest
adjectives ending in one vowel + consonant	double the final consonant *	big → bigger → biggest hot → hotter → hottest

* But we do not double -w: slow → slower → slowest

3 Spelling rules for adverbs

To make an adverb, we often add -ly to an adjective.

Adjective	Rule	Examples
most adjectives	add -ly	slow → slowly quick → quickly
adjectives ending in -y	change -y to -i	angry → angrily easy → easily

4 Spelling rules for present simple verbs (he, she, it)

Verb	Rule	Examples
most verbs	add -s	read → reads sleep → sleeps
verbs ending in consonant + -y	change -y to -i	fly → flies study → studies
verbs ending in vowel + -y	add -s	buy → buys play → plays
verbs ending in -ch, -sh, -ss, -s or -x	add -es	watch → watches finish → finishes miss → misses fix → fixes
verbs ending in -o	add -es	go → goes do → does

5 Spelling rules for verbs + *-ing*

Verb	Rule	Examples
most verbs	add *-ing*	sleep → sleep**ing** work → work**ing**
verbs ending in *-e*	take away the *-e*	live → liv**ing** dance → danc**ing**
verbs ending in *-ee*	add *-ing*	see → see**ing** agree → agree**ing**
verbs ending in *-ie*	change *-ie* to *-y*	l**ie** → l**ying** d**ie** → d**ying**
verbs ending in one vowel + consonant	double the final consonant *	st**op** → sto**pping** sw**im** → swi**mming**
verbs ending in two vowels + consonant	add *-ing*	r**ain** → rain**ing** r**ead** → read**ing**

* But we do not double the final consonant if the last part of the word is not stressed:
begin → *begi**nn**ing* BUT *open* → *open**ing***
And we do not double *-w*: *snow* → *sno**w**ing*

6 Spelling rules for verbs + *-ed*

Verb	Rule	Examples
most verbs	add *-ed*	ask → ask**ed** help → help**ed**
verbs ending in *-e* or *-ee*	add *-d*	arrive → arrive**d** agree → agree**d**
verbs ending in consonant + *-y*	change *-y* to *-i*	stud**y** → stud**ied** tr**y** → tr**ied**
verbs ending in vowel + *-y*	add *-ed*	pl**ay** → play**ed** enj**oy** → enjoy**ed**
verbs ending in one vowel + consonant	double the final consonant *	st**op** → sto**pped** pl**an** → pla**nned**
verbs ending in two vowels + consonant	add *-ed*	r**ain** → rain**ed** rep**eat** → repeat**ed**

* But we do not double the final consonant if the last part of the word is not stressed:
prefer → *prefe**rr**ed* BUT *answer* → *answe**r**ed*
And we do not double *-w*: *snow* → *sno**w**ed*

7 Spelling rules for adjectives ending in *-y*

We can make some adjectives by adding *-y* to a noun.

Noun	Rule	Examples
most nouns	add *-y*	rain → rain**y** cloud → cloud**y**
nouns ending in *-e*	take away the *-e*	noise → nois**y** smoke → smok**y**
nouns ending in one vowel + consonant	double the final consonant	s**un** → su**nny** f**og** → fo**ggy**

8 State verbs

be	hear	mean	see	understand
believe	know	need	smell	want
hate	like	prefer	taste	wish
have	love	remember	think	

9 Verbs followed by *-ing* form

begin	finish	like	miss	stop
continue	hate	love	prefer	suggest
enjoy	imagine	mind	start	

10 Verbs followed by *to*-infinitive

agree	expect	learn	plan	try
ask	forget	need	promise	want
decide	hope	offer	refuse	

11 Short forms of verbs

In spoken English, we usually use the short forms of verbs (*'s*, *haven' t*, *didn' t*, etc). We sometimes use them in written English, too: *He's late.*   *They **haven't** got a car.*   *We **didn't** go to the party.*

Affirmative	Negative	
'm (= am)	isn't (= is not)	didn't (= did not)
's (= is)	aren't (= are not)	won't (= will not)
're (= are)	wasn't (= was not)	can't (= cannot)
've (= have)	weren't (= were not)	couldn't (= could not)
's (= has)	haven't (= have not)	mustn't (= must not)
'll (= will)	hasn't (= has not)	shouldn't (= should not)
'd (= would)	don't (= do not)	mightn't (= might not)
	doesn't (= does not)	

Affirmative short forms

● We can use *'s* (= *is* or *has*) after pronouns, question words or nouns and names:
She's at college.   *What's that?*   *Our flat's got a balcony.*   *Kate's got a red car.*

● We can use *'re* (= *are*) and *'ve* (= *have*) after pronouns:
We're students.   *They've never been to London.*

But we do not use them after nouns, names and question words:
Those boys are students at my college.   *Liz and Anna are very good dancers.*
Mr and Mrs Harrison have been very kind to me.

● We often use *'ll* and *'d* after pronouns: *We'll be there at six.*   *I'd like to buy this computer game.*

● We do not use affirmative short forms at the end of a sentence:
A: Are you ready?   B: Yes, we are. (Not ~~Yes, we're.~~)

Negative short forms

● We can use negative short forms after any pronouns, nouns or names:
*She **isn't** at home.*   *My cousins **don't** live here.*   *Emma **didn't** come to the party.*

● With *is not* and *are not*, two negative short forms are possible: *isn' t/'s not* and *aren' t/'re not*:
*He **isn't** coming. / He's **not** coming.*   *We **aren't** leaving. / We're **not** leaving.*
But we can only say *I'm not* (Not ~~I amn't~~).

● We can use negative short forms at the end of a sentence:
*A: Are you ready?   B: No, we **aren't**.*

12 Irregular verbs

Infinitive	Past simple	Past participle
be	was/were	been
beat	beat	beaten
become	became	become
begin	began	begun
bite	bit	bitten
blow	blew	blown
break	broke	broken
bring	brought	brought
build	built	built
buy	bought	bought
catch	caught	caught
choose	chose	chosen
come	came	come
cost	cost	cost
cut	cut	cut
do	did	done
draw	drew	drawn
dream	dreamed/dreamt	dreamed/dreamt
drink	drank	drunk
drive	drove	driven
eat	ate	eaten
fall	fell	fallen
feel	felt	felt
fight	fought	fought
find	found	found
fly	flew	flown
forget	forgot	forgotten
get	got	got
give	gave	given
go	went	gone
grow	grew	grown
hang	hung	hung
have	had	had
hear	heard	heard
hit	hit	hit
hold	held	held
hurt	hurt	hurt
keep	kept	kept
know	knew	known
learn	learned/learnt	learned/learnt
leave	left	left

Infinitive	Past simple	Past participle
lend	lent	lent
let	let	let
lie	lay	lain
lose	lost	lost
make	made	made
mean	meant	meant
meet	met	met
pay	paid	paid
put	put	put
read	read	read
ride	rode	ridden
ring	rang	rung
run	ran	run
say	said	said
see	saw	seen
sell	sold	sold
send	sent	sent
set	set	set
show	showed	shown
shut	shut	shut
sing	sang	sung
sit	sat	sat
sleep	slept	slept
smell	smelled/smelt	smelled/smelt
speak	spoke	spoken
spell	spelled/spelt	spelled/spelt
spend	spent	spent
stand	stood	stood
steal	stole	stolen
swim	swam	swum
take	took	taken
teach	taught	taught
tell	told	told
think	thought	thought
throw	threw	thrown
understand	understood	understood
wake	woke	woken
wear	wore	worn
win	won	won
write	wrote	written

13 Adjective + preposition

afraid of	different from	interested in	proud of
angry about (something)	excited about	kind to	sorry about/for
angry with (someone)	famous for	married to	sure of
bad at	fed up with	nervous about	surprised at/by
brilliant at	frightened of	nice to	terrible at
careful with	full of	pleased with	tired of
crazy about	good at	polite to	worried about

14 Common phrasal verbs

break down = if a car or machine breaks down, it stops working

carry on = to continue doing something

come back = to return

come round = to visit someone

drive off = if a car drives off, it leaves

find out = to get information about something

get back = to return

get off = to leave a bus, train, plane, etc.

get on = to walk onto a bus, train, plane, etc.

get up = to wake up and get out of bed

give up = to stop doing something

go away = to leave a place or person

go back = to return

go on = to continue doing something

go out = to leave your house to do something you enjoy

hurry up = to do something more quickly

keep on = to continue doing something

lie down = when you lie down, your body is flat on a bed, on the floor, etc.

look after = to take care of someone or something

look at = to turn your eyes towards something, so that you can see it

look for = to try to find someone or something

look out = used to warn someone of danger

look up = to find information in a book, on a computer, etc.

put on = to put clothes on your body

ring up = to telephone someone

set off = to leave and start going somewhere

sit down = to lower yourself down so that you are sitting

stand up = to get up so that you are standing after you have been sitting or lying down

stay in = to stay in your home and not go out

stay up = to not go to bed

take off = to remove something

throw away = to get rid of something that you do not want

try on = to put on a piece of clothing to find out if it fits or if you like it

turn down = to make a machine produce less heat, sound, etc.

turn off = to make a machine, light, etc. stop working

turn on = to make a machine, light, etc. start working

turn up = to make a machine produce more heat, sound, etc.

wake up = to stop sleeping, or to make someone stop sleeping

wash up = to wash the plates, dishes, etc. after a meal

write down = to write something on a piece of paper, especially so that you do not forget it

Index

The numbers in this index are unit numbers (not page numbers).

Answer key

In your answers, you can use the full or short forms of verbs, e.g. *She is coming* or *She's coming*. Both forms are generally correct. There are only a few occasions when it is not possible to use the short form of a verb. See Appendix 7 on short forms.

Unit 1

1a

−s: bags, birthdays, brothers, coats, euros, oranges, pens, places, programmes, tables, toys, trees

−es: *addresses*, boxes, brushes, buses, churches, dishes, dresses, foxes, sandwiches, tomatoes, watches, wishes

1b

Singular	Plural	Singular	Plural
beach	*beaches*	shelf	shelves
holiday	holidays	shoe	shoes
loaf	loaves	foot	feet
man	men	eye	eyes
dictionary	dictionaries	glass	glasses
person	people	potato	potatoes

Unit 2

2a

a		an	
bottle	map	*animal*	ice cream
CD	neighbour	answer	insect
desk	photo	arm	island
film	ruler	aunt	octopus
goal	ship	e-mail	omelette
holiday	town	envelope	office
key	visitor	exam	umbrella
lemon	window	exercise	uncle

2b

1 a 2 an 3 a 4 an 5 an 6 a 7 an 8 a 9 a 10 an

2c

1 a 2 an 3 a 4 a 5 a 6 a 7 an 8 an 9 a, a 10 a 11 a 12 an, a 13 a 14 a, an 15 a

There isn't a basketball or a wallet in the picture.

Unit 3

3a

1 photos 2 people 3 an 4 Faces 5 a 6 the photos 7 the 8 the flowers 9 a 10 the

3b

1 the 2 an 3 − 4 the 5 the 6 a 7 a 8 the 9 − 10 The

Unit 4

4a

bread	U	chair	C	juice	U
CD	C	umbrella	C	idea	C
soup	U	rain	U	bus	C
information	U	child	C	air	U
bottle	C	T-shirt	C	book	C
oil	U	tea	U	job	C
friend	C	café	C	fun	U
cheese	U	homework	U	programme	C
food	U	milk	U	song	C
cup	C	music	U	snow	U
honey	U	flower	C	popcorn	U
shirt	C	luck	U	box	C

4b

1 − 2 − 3 − 4 an 5 a 6 a 7 a 8 − 9 − 10 −

Unit 5

5a

1 some 2 some 3 an 4 some 5 some 6 a

5b

1 any 2 some 3 any 4 some 5 any 6 some

5c

1 any 2 some 3 any 4 a 5 any 6 some 7 a 8 some

5d

1 any 2 any 3 no 4 any 5 no 6 no 7 any 8 no 9 any 10 no

5e

1 any 2 no 3 a 4 some 5 some 6 any 7 no 8 no

Unit 6

6a

1 glass 2 bowl 3 bottle 4 tube 5 can 6 slice 7 carton 8 jar

6b

1 piece 2 tins 3 piece 4 pieces 5 kilos 6 piece

Unit 7

7a

1 many 2 many 3 much 4 much 5 many 6 much 7 much 8 many

7b

1 How much 2 How much 3 How many 4 How much 5 How many 6 How many 7 How much 8 How many

7c

1 How many 2 much 3 much 4 more 5 more 6 more 7 more 8 How much

7d

1 more 2 much 3 many 4 many 5 much 6 many 7 More 8 more

Unit 8

8a
1 a few 2 a few 3 a little 4 A few 5 a little 6 a little
7 a few 8 a little 9 a few 10 a little

8b
1 a lot of/lots of sweets 2 a little water 3 a little chocolate
4 a lot of/lots of ice 5 a few minutes 6 a little sugar
7 a few CDs 8 a lot of/lots of words 9 a lot of/lots of milk
10 a few messages 11 a lot of/lots of e-mails

8c
1 a little 2 lots of 3 a lot of 4 a few 5 a lot of 6 a lot of

Unit 9

9a
1 All the cups are dirty.
2 All the exams start at 9.00.
3 All the players in the team are important.
4 All the tickets here are expensive.
5 All the rooms in the hotel have a television.
6 All the lights in the flat are on.
7 All the students will take the test.
8 All the buses stop here.

9b
1 every 2 all 3 all the 4 every 5 every 6 all

9c
1 all 2 every 3 Every 4 all 5 every 6 all

Check 1 Nouns and determiners

1
1 some 2 every 3 any 4 dictionaries 5 a few

2
6 many 7 no 8 much 9 an 10 the

3
11 every 12 slice 13 some 14 milk 15 a little 16 rice
17 potatoes 18 lots of 19 an orange 20 bar

Unit 10

10a
1 He 2 It 3 I 4 We 5 She 6 You

10b
1 them 2 us 3 you 4 him 5 me 6 it 7 you 8 her

10c
1 I 2 He 3 him 4 them 5 We 6 me 7 They 8 us

Unit 11

11a
1 d 2 b 3 e 4 a 5 c

11b
1 Its/My 2 my 3 our 4 your 5 Their 6 Her 7 his 8 My

Unit 12

12a
1 the boys' names 2 Sarah and John's aunt 3 the cat's basket
4 those ladies' bags 5 Ben's birthday 6 my friends' house
7 Lisa's phone number 8 Mr Smith's shop 9 my parents'
bedroom 10 Jo's book 11 my cousins' dog 12 Ian's car
13 men's clothes

12b
1 Where's Andrew's wallet?
2 What are those men's names?
3 Are these your friends' photos?
4 The dog's name's Jet.
5 Where are Amy and Kim's CDs?
6 That's our neighbours' cat.

12c
1 Jamie and Craig's 2 dad's 3 children's 4 mum's 5 parents'
6 brother's

12d
1 mother's 2 Michael and Liz's 3 brother's 4 parents'
5 cousins' 6 father's

Unit 13

13a
1 screen 2 of the corridor 3 of the class 4 window
5 of the film 6 centre

13b
1 kitchen door 2 living room curtains 3 top of the stairs
4 back of the house 5 bedroom window 6 side of the house

Unit 14

14a
1 hers 2 ours 3 yours 4 his 5 theirs 6 mine 7 hers
8 yours

14b
1 ours 2 Her 3 Yours 4 her 5 theirs 6 ours 7 your 8 yours

Unit 15

15a
1 these 2 that 3 Those 4 this 5 those 6 these 7 This
8 that

15b
1 this, that 2 those, these 3 that, That

15c
1 this match 2 that match 3 That cake 4 This cake
5 these tennis lessons 6 those tennis lessons 7 those trips
8 these trips

Unit 16

16a
1 Emma's 2 Mark's 3 Rebecca and Kirsty's 4 Laura's
5 Sam's 6 Nick and Justin's

16b
1 my parents' 2 my cousins' 3 my brother's 4 my aunt's
5 my friend's

Unit 17

17a

1 those ones   2 these ones   3 this one   4 that one
5 pink ones

17b

1 the ones near the Italian café
2 the one with a/the blue table and chairs
3 The ones with the plants
4 the one with the blue door
5 the one opposite the bookshop

Unit 18

18a

1 everywhere   2 something   3 somebody   4 somewhere
5 everything   6 everybody   7 Somebody   8 everywhere

18b

1 somewhere   2 somebody   3 everywhere   4 something
5 everybody

Unit 19

19a

1 anybody   2 nowhere   3 nothing   4 anywhere   5 no one
6 anything   7 anywhere   8 nothing

19b

1 nobody   2 anybody   3 anything   4 anywhere   5 nothing
6 nowhere

Check 2 Pronouns and possessives

1

1 your   2 somewhere   3 brother's   4 These   5 sisters'

2

6 he   7 him   8 nobody   9 Everybody   10 his

3

11 my father's   12 back of   13 ones   14 theirs   15 anything

4

16 Her   17 one   18 They   19 mine   20 of

Unit 20

20a

1 the   2 an   3 the   4 a   5 the   6 a   7 a   8 the   9 a   10 an
11 a   12 a

20b

1 the   2 the   3 a   4 a   5 a   6 a   7 a   8 a   9 The   10 The
11 The   12 The

Unit 21

21a

1 the   2 an   3 a   4 The   5 the   6 a   7 the   8 an   9 the   10 a

21b

1 the   2 The   3 the   4 the   5 the   6 a   7 a   8 the

Unit 22

22a

1 a   2 the   3 a   4 The   5 the   6 the

22b

1 a   2 the   3 the   4 a   5 the   6 the   7 the   8 the

22c

1 the   2 ✓   3 the   4 ✓   5 ✓   6 the

22d

1 the   2 a   3 –   4 –   5 The   6 an   7 –   8 –

Check 3 Articles

1

1 a   2 a   3 the   4 the   5 an

2

6 a   7 a   8 the   9 the   10 a   11 the

3

12 an   13 the   14 The   15 a   16 The   17 the

4

18 the   19 a   20 –   21 –   22 The   23 a   24 –   25 –

Unit 23

23a

1 We live in a quiet street.   5 Emma and Sarah are late.
2 These jeans are cheap.   6 They've got a small shop.
3 My notebook is blue.   7 That bag is expensive.
4 My brother likes big cities. 8 Zoe loves red roses.

23b

1 delicious   2 green   3 a fantastic   4 heavy   5 an old
6 a black   7 a great   8 nice

Unit 24

24a

1 younger   2 prettier   3 darker   4 easier   5 bigger   6 safer
7 funnier   8 better

24b

1 more exciting   2 more comfortable   3 more expensive
4 more intelligent   5 more interesting   6 more difficult
7 more dangerous   8 more popular

24c

1 Victoria, longer than Parkway
2 Victoria, colder than Parkway
3 Parkway, better
4 Parkway, bigger than, Victoria
5 Victoria, more crowded than Parkway
6 Parkway, more expensive than, Victoria

Unit 25

25a

1 the cheapest   2 the most difficult   3 The prettiest
4 the most interesting   5 The best   6 the funniest
7 the biggest   8 the most expensive

25b

1 The oldest   2 the highest   3 the sunniest   4 the deepest
5 the longest   6 the most dangerous   7 the farthest/furthest
8 the most expensive

Unit 26

26a

1a warmer than   1b the coldest   1c the warmest
2a more interesting than   2b the most boring
2c the most interesting

26b

1 cheaper than   2 nicer   3 more comfortable   4 the worst
5 the best   6 the most popular

Unit 27

27a

1 a lovely big garden   2 a pretty pink T-shirt   3 some
awful orange trousers   4 a small black cat   5 a beautiful
white beach   6 some big green bags

27b

1 short white   2 big green   3 nice red   4 amazing little
5 beautiful big   6 nice black   7 nice short   8 pretty blue
9 long blue   10 lovely blue

Unit 28

28a

1 slowly   2 clearly   3 noisily   4 easily   5 quickly   6 perfectly
7 loudly   8 carefully   9 nervously   10 angrily

28b

1 She plays badly.   4 I learn fast.
2 He drives dangerously.   5 You write well.
3 They work hard.   6 She dances wonderfully.

28c

1 busy   2 brilliant   3 beautiful   4 suddenly   5 quietly   6 nice
7 carefully   8 safely

Unit 29

29a

1 the most beautifully   2 more clearly than   3 the most
dangerously   4 the worst   5 harder than   6 faster than

29b

1 the most easily   2 more easily than   3 better than
4 the best   5 faster than   6 the fastest   7 more carefully than
8 the most carefully   9 more calmly than   10 the most calmly

Robert would be the best leader.

Unit 30

30a

1 They're too expensive.   4 I'm too tired.
2 It's too sweet.   5 She's too busy.
3 It's too long.

30b

1 'm not good enough   2 'm not clever enough   3 isn't fast
enough   4 isn't tall enough   5 isn't big enough

30c

1 too short   2 too shy   3 not old enough   4 not fit enough
5 too difficult   6 not strong enough

Unit 31

31a

1 Joe and I sometimes go swimming.
2 Our street is always quiet.
3 My father sometimes plays football with me.
4 We often go to the beach.
5 My brother usually gets up at six.
6 I never drink coffee.
7 Our holidays in Spain are always wonderful.
8 Jason usually goes to bed at nine.

31b

1 My friends don't usually go home on the bus.
2 Does Ashley sometimes phone you?
3 The tickets aren't usually expensive.
4 My mum doesn't often work on Saturdays.
5 Is your sister always funny?
6 Do you always go out on Saturdays?
7 The train isn't often crowded.
8 Do they often visit their cousins?

31c

1 Kelly doesn't often write for the school magazine.
2 Mark writes for the school magazine every month. / Every
   month Mark writes for the school magazine.
3 Kelly does karate every week. / Every week Kelly does
   karate.
4 Mark never does karate.
5 Kelly never plays the piano.
6 Mark plays the piano every day. / Every day Mark plays the
   piano.
7 Kelly's often ill.
8 Mark isn't often ill.

Check 4 Adjectives and adverbs

1

1 I sometimes go to London.
2 This programme is awful.
3 Luke is never late.
4 We always have dinner at eight.
5 Kate has got long dark hair.

2

6 are too small   7 more   8 aren't wide enough   9 wide feet
10 little black

3

11 careful   12 loudly   13 carefully   14 loud   15 beautifully

4

16 the laziest   17 the worst   18 better   19 more interesting
20 the hardest

Unit 32

32a

1 am 2 am 3 is 4 are 5 am 6 are 7 is 8 are 9 am 10 is

32b

1 we aren't late. We're early.

2 they aren't from Italy. They're from Poland.

3 I'm not ill. I'm fine.

4 he isn't a journalist. He's a doctor.

5 you aren't fat. You're thin.

32c

1 Are you 2 I'm not 3 Is Kim 4 Are Laura and Kim
5 they aren't 6 is your gig 7 it isn't 8 is it 9 are you
10 I am / we are

32d

1 's 2 'm 3 's 4 isn't 5 are 6 aren't 7 are 8 Is

Unit 33

33a

1 I've got a comb.   6 She's got a sister.

2 She's got fair hair.   7 They've got a cat.

3 He's got a cold.   8 We've got £50.

4 We've got them.   9 They've got a little boy.

5 I've got a headache.   10 It's got a cinema.

33b

1 's got, hasn't got 2 haven't got, 've got 3 haven't got, 've
got 4 have got, haven't got 5 've got, haven't got

33c

1 Have you got a headache?

2 Has your brother got a bike?

3 Have they got a computer?

4 Has Emma got brown eyes?

5 Has he got a cold?

6 Have Mick and Anna got a car?

33d

1 've got 2 Have, got 3 haven't 4 Has, got 5 Have, got
6 have 7 haven't got 8 's got 9 Has, got 10 hasn't 11 's got
12 haven't got

Unit 34

34a

I/you/we/they	he/she/it	I/you/we/they	he/she/it
finish	finishes	stay	stays
teach	teaches	study	studies
try	tries	give	gives
like	likes	say	says
wash	washes	mix	mixes
worry	worries	wear	wears
go	goes	touch	touches
miss	misses	listen	listens
start	starts	cry	cries
carry	carries	live	lives
lie	lies	want	wants

34b

1 go 2 goes 3 like 4 miss 5 write 6 visit 7 comes 8 have

34c

1 brings 2 wears 3 helps 4 cut 5 get 6 go

34d

1 My friends often buy clothes.

2 I never forget my friends' birthdays.

3 Clare drinks coffee every morning. / Every morning Clare
drinks coffee.

4 They always have lunch at 12.00.

5 We go to the cinema every week. / Every week we go to the
cinema.

34e

Students' own answers

Unit 35

35a

1 doesn't live 2 doesn't open 3 don't go 4 doesn't like
5 don't know 6 don't sell 7 don't visit 8 don't do

35b

1 don't read 2 doesn't walk 3 don't go out 4 doesn't need
5 doesn't speak 6 don't drink 7 don't want 8 don't know

35c

1 don't understand 2 doesn't say 3 don't talk 4 don't know
5 don't want

Unit 36

36a

1 Does that shop sell cold drinks?

2 Where does your sister work?

3 Do they play rock music?

4 Do we need any sugar?

5 When does he play football?

6 What do you want?

36b

1 they don't 2 I/we don't 3 he doesn't 4 he does
5 he doesn't 6 I/we do

36c

Students' own answers

36d

1 Where do you live?

2 Do your parents have a blue Audi?

3 Does your dad wear glasses?

4 Do you and Lisa play tennis together?

5 When do you play?

Check 5 Present simple

1

1 aren't 2 's 3 hasn't got 4 'm 5 've got 6 's 7 've got

2

8 What is your name?   12 Where do they live?

9 Have you got a map?   13 Rob doesn't play tennis.

10 We often go to the park.   14 I don't drink coffee.

11 He doesn't wear glasses.

3

15 go   16 cycle   17 doesn't come   18 doesn't like   19 prefers

4

20 does   21 does   22 has   23 Do   24 do   25 have

Unit 37

37a

Infinitive	-*ing* form	Infinitive	-*ing* form
stop	*stopping*	lie	lying
get	getting	win	winning
smile	smiling	make	making
ask	asking	wear	wearing
drive	driving	ride	riding
dream	dreaming	watch	watching
hit	hitting	jump	jumping
shut	shutting	drink	drinking

37b

1 are cooking   2 's playing   3 's singing   4 are dancing
5 are swimming   6 are sitting   7 's telling   8 are listening
9 's taking   10 's running

37c

1 They're lying on the grass.
2 She's writing a postcard
3 They're watching a DVD.
4 He's having breakfast.
5 They're playing volleyball.

37d

1 's talking   2 's ordering   3 are moving   4 're putting
5 'm listening   6 're sitting

Unit 38

38a

1 aren't talking   2 aren't staying   3 isn't wearing
4 'm not enjoying   5 aren't having   6 isn't working

38b

1 Is Adam using his laptop?
2 Where are you going?
3 Why are Kate and Lisa laughing?
4 Am I sitting in your chair?
5 Is it raining?
6 Why is he looking at me?
7 Is Emma working?
8 Why are you wearing my sunglasses?

38c

1 Are you watching TV?   I am/we are
2 Is Rob watching with you?   he isn't
3 Are they playing tennis?   they aren't
4 Are they training for their race?   they are
5 Are Sam and Tim training with them?   they aren't
6 Is he revising for his exams?   he is

38d

1 I am   2 isn't moving   3 aren't doing   4 's Jack doing
5 Is he playing   6 he isn't

Unit 39

39a

1 e   2 b   3 a   4 d   5 c

39b

1 's working, works   2 'm not wearing, don't wear
3 'm not watching, don't watch   4 run, 're running
5 don't win, aren't winning

39c

1 He's looking for   2 Kate doesn't like   3 They're getting
4 are you reading   5 I don't believe

39d

1 's having   2 's helping   3 doesn't know   4 helps
5 Are you looking   6 keep

39e

1 don't live   2 get   3 have   4 hate   5 's painting   6 's making
7 's playing   8 Do you need

Check 6   Present simple or present continuous

1

1 Is Mark having   2 's working   3 isn't using   4 are sitting
5 Are you listening   6 'm reading

2

7 are, doing   8 'm cooking   9 Are, watching   10 aren't
watching   11 's painting   12 Is, helping

3

13 are you talking   14 I don't need   15 We go   16 Do you
understand   17 He's getting   18 He hates   19 are you laughing
20 They do

Unit 40

40a

1 were   2 was   3 was   4 was   5 were   6 was   7 were   8 were
9 was   10 was

40b

1 wasn't   2 was   3 weren't   4 were   5 was   6 wasn't

40c

1 Where were you?
2 Was the museum open?
3 Was Sam with you?
4 Why was he late?
5 Were you annoyed?
6 Why were the tickets expensive?

40d

1 it was   2 she wasn't   3 we were   4 they weren't   5 he was
6 he wasn't

40e

1 were   2 Was   3 was   4 were   5 Were   6 weren't   7 were
8 were   9 was   10 was

Unit 41

41a

Infinitive	Past simple	Infinitive	Past simple
talk	*talked*	enjoy	enjoyed
listen	listened	marry	married
carry	carried	rain	rained
dance	danced	live	lived
look	looked	rob	robbed
stop	stopped	want	wanted
hope	hoped	plan	planned
ask	asked	wash	washed

41b

1 I cycled to college   2 She watched television   3 They visited us   4 I tidied my room   5 He phoned me   6 You worked hard
7 I walked to work   8 He stayed with us

41c

1 helped   2 designed   3 performed   4 played   5 organised
6 visited

41d

1 completed   2 trained   3 pulled   4 practised   5 travelled
6 tried   7 succeeded   8 finished

41e

1 answered   2 studied   3 stayed   4 moved   5 wanted
6 decided

Unit 42

42a

Infinitive	Past simple	Infinitive	Past simple
come	*came*	know	knew
put	put	understand	understood
get	got	do	did
tell	told	speak	spoke
cut	cut	feel	felt
think	thought	write	wrote
let	let	sing	sang
bring	brought	buy	bought
keep	kept	fall	fell
win	won	forget	forgot

42b

1 had   2 met   3 found   4 sat   5 gave   6 paid   7 left   8 went

42c

1 We swam in the sea.
2 Tim took some photos.
3 I read a magazine.
4 We ate our sandwiches.
5 I ran along the beach.
6 We had a great time.

42d

1 bought   2 took   3 taught   4 went   5 saw   6 met   7 slept
8 woke up

42e

1 made   2 drove   3 spent   4 spoke   5 sent   6 felt   7 had
8 went

Unit 43

43a

1 didn't bring   2 didn't speak   3 didn't ask   4 didn't make
5 didn't think   6 didn't have   7 didn't read   8 didn't send

43b

1 She didn't write (to me)   2 You didn't spend much
3 He didn't call (me)   4 They didn't go on holiday
5 We didn't live in London   6 Our team didn't win
7 We didn't watch TV   8 I didn't see her

43c

1 Did you go anywhere?
2 Did Jack and Lucy come with you?
3 How did you get there?
4 Where did you meet Nina?
5 Did you have a good time?

43d

1 I/we did   2 she didn't   3 it didn't   4 we did   5 they did

43e

Students' own answers

43f

1 did you leave   2 didn't stop   3 Did you come   4 didn't
5 Did somebody meet   6 didn't have

Unit 44

44a

1 week   2 yesterday   3 days   4 last   5 months   6 ago

44b

1 When we came   2 when I was   3 When I was   4 when we
lived   5 when the book became

Check 7 Past simple

1

1 weren't   2 Did you talk   3 left   4 missed   5 Was Adam
6 bought   7 helped   8 had

2

9 I/we did   10 it was   11 we didn't   12 they weren't
13 she wasn't   14 she did   15 I/we did

3

16 yesterday   17 ago   18 year   19 last   20 when

4

21 did, enjoy   22 loved   23 saw   24 tried   25 were

Unit 45

45a

1 was raining   2 weren't wearing   3 were talking
4 wasn't listening   5 was telling   6 was standing
7 was carrying   8 wasn't crying

45b

1 Why were you laughing?
2 Was it snowing?
3 Was Sarah showing you her photos?
4 Where were they going?
5 Was Tom having lunch?
6 Was Amy wearing her new shoes?

45c
1 I was 2 she wasn't 3 she was 4 they weren't 5 he was

45d
1 While, were playing, was reading
2 was shining, while, were climbing
3 wasn't watching, while, was talking
4 While, was doing, were cleaning

45e
1 was talking 2 was thinking 3 were you doing
4 were getting 5 was cooking 6 was moving

Unit 46
46a
1 were driving 2 started 3 stole 4 were going
5 was standing 6 saw

46b
1 met, was studying 2 was working, phoned 3 Were you
going, saw 4 saw, wasn't watching 5 Was Lucy having, left
6 were driving, stopped

46c
1 was studying 2 heard 3 didn't come 4 was staying 5 met
6 gave

46d
1 heard 2 were, going 3 saw 4 was cycling 5 fell
6 stopped 7 saw 8 took 9 met 10 went 11 Was, waiting
12 arrived

Check 8 Past continuous and past simple
1
1 Were you 2 were sitting 3 were swimming 4 Was Adam
5 was working 6 Were they 7 were revising

2
8 played 9 told 10 were you walking 11 saw 12 was playing
13 arrived 14 was waiting

3
15 when 16 was 17 while 18 were 19 Were

4
20 was waiting 21 asked 22 gave 23 joined 24 saw
25 was doing

Unit 47
47a
1 've moved 2 've mended 3 's lost 4 's broken 5 've taken
6 's stopped 7 's locked 8 've brought

47b
1 haven't come 2 hasn't invited 3 haven't seen
4 hasn't packed 5 haven't turned 6 haven't read

47c
1 Have they had breakfast? they haven't
2 Has Emma got dressed? she hasn't.
3 Has Sam made any coffee? he has.
4 Has he walked the dog? he hasn't.
5 Have you finished your breakfast? I/we have.
6 Have you had a shower? I/we haven't.

47d
1 's hurt 2 Have I broken 3 Have you hurt 4 haven't
5 haven't brought 6 haven't looked

Unit 48
48a
1 's already washed 2 've already asked 3 've already left
4 've already lent 5 've already had 6 've already met
7 've already bought 8 's already locked

48b
1 She's already phoned Nicole.
2 She hasn't written to Kate yet.
3 She hasn't finished her project yet.
4 She's already picked up her/the jacket from the cleaner's.
5 She hasn't ironed her/the skirt yet.
6 She's already washed her/the T-shirts.

48c
1 Have you planned the journey yet?
2 Have Sam and Joe booked the hotel yet?
3 Has Sam told his parents yet?
4 Have you learnt any Spanish yet?
5 Has Joe packed his bag yet?
6 Have you found your passport yet?

48d
1 've just got 2 have just come 3 've just remembered
4 's just asked 5 've just arranged 6 's just called

48e
1 already 2 yet 3 yet 4 just 5 yet 6 already 7 just 8 yet

Unit 49
49a
1 's played, 's never sung/hasn't sung 2 have never ridden/
haven't ridden, 've driven 3 've ridden, 've played 4 've never
had/haven't had

49b
1 Have you ever been late for a meeting?
2 Has the director ever spoken to you?
3 Have you ever visited this website?
4 Have Kim and Zoe ever had lunch with you?
5 Have you ever been to that café?
6 Has Tom ever phoned you?

49c
1 gone 2 been 3 been 4 gone 5 been 6 gone 7 gone
8 been

49d
1 've never heard 2 Have you ever been 3 's been
4 has happened 5 's never shown 6 've gone

Unit 50
50a

for		since	
a few minutes	ten days	half past five	this morning
a long time	three weeks	last week	Tuesday
centuries	twelve years	March	yesterday
eight months	two hours	midnight	2004

50b

1 's lived, since   2 've had, for   3 've been, since   4 's had, for
5 've known, for   6 's loved, since   7 have been, since
8 's worked, for

50c

1 How long have you had your car?
2 How long have you lived in the country?
3 How long has this college been open?
4 How long has it had these sports facilities?
5 How long have you known Adam and Scott?
6 How long have they been in the football team?
7 How long has your brother worked here?
8 How long have you had your dog?

50d

1 for   2 since   3 long   4 since   5 for   6 since

50e

Students' own answers

Unit 51

51a

1 Have you seen, Did you see   2 I read, I've read   3 We
haven't finished, We didn't finish   4 They went, They've gone
5 He broke, He's broken   6 They've moved, They moved

51b

1 went   2 phoned   3 saw   4 's just come   5 was   6 's gone
7 've made   8 did you make

51c

1 I saw   2 Mum's tidied   3 She's put   4 He left   5 Have you
been   6 I had

51d

1 had   2 moved   3 joined   4 've worked   5 've learned/learnt
6 've been   7 went   8 met

Check 9   Present perfect

1

1 She has just left.
2 Have they told her yet?
3 We have already had lunch.
4 Have you ever been to Ireland?
5 He has not phoned yet.
6 I have never tried Indian food.
7 Has Matt ever ridden a horse?

2

8 gone   9 since   10 never   11 just   12 for   13 since   14 been
15 for

3

16 Have you moved   17 have   18 's given   19 've ordered
20 hasn't come

4

21 've been   22 've met   23 's lived   24 had   25 came

Unit 52

52a

1 'm going to visit   2 'm going to see   3 're going to have
4 's going to come   5 are going to take   6 's going to help
7 're going to use   8 'm going to ask

52b

1 isn't going to get up   2 aren't going to have   3 aren't going
to stay   4 isn't going to keep   5 'm not going to work   6 aren't
going to paint

52c

1 Is she going to stay with you on Sunday?
2 Are your friends going to have a party?
3 Are we going to tell Ryan about Becky?
4 What are you going to do in the summer?
5 Is Matt going to learn to drive next year?
6 Where are they going to stay?
7 Are you going to see Justin tomorrow?
8 Is he going to move here in September?

52d

1 Is she going to come   2 isn't   3 are you going to do
4 're going to take   5 aren't going to stay   6 're going to go

Unit 53

53a

1 won't know   2 will love   3 won't win   4 won't get
5 'll lend   6 'll have

53b

1 will, You'll remember   2 won't, I'll need   3 will, She'll bring
4 won't, We'll see   5 will, You'll have

53c

1 I won't eat   2 I'll talk   3 I won't have   4 I won't get   5 I'll get
6 I'll wait

Unit 54

54a

1 I'll call   2 I'm going to have   3 I'll look   4 I'll go   5 I'm going
to do   6 I'm going to buy   7 I'll get   8 I'm going to wear

54b

1 'm going to have   2 'll think   3 'll come   4 'm going to get
5 'll read   6 'm going to sell   7 'm going to visit   8 'll ask

54c

1 'll come   2 'll ask   3 'll borrow   4 'm going to bring
5 'm going to drive   6 'm going to go

Unit 55

55a

1 Is Kate driving   2 isn't working   3 are you doing   4 'm not
doing   5 are coming   6 are we having

55b

1 They aren't coming   2 She won't listen   3 Adam's meeting
4 You'll enjoy   5 Nobody will take   6 We're moving   7 Craig
won't know   8 We're going

Unit 56

56a

1 leaves 2 starts 3 opens 4 is 5 stops 6 does it finish
7 closes 8 does the film begin

56b

1 do they finish 2 I'm going 3 Are you getting 4 The bus
leaves 5 arrives 6 We're staying 7 we're getting
8 We're coming

Check 10 Future forms

1

1 will 2 'll 3 does 4 Are 5 to 6 're 7 going 8 's

2

9 I'm going to see 10 They're performing 11 The exhibition
finishes 12 I'll use 13 does the film start 14 We're leaving
15 The bank closes

3

16 'm going to see 17 'll tell 18 are you going to meet
19 'll call 20 'll give

4

21 open 22 're getting 23 arrives 24 're having 25 'll have

Unit 57

57a

1 can drive 2 can't see 3 can't understand 4 can't come
5 can speak 6 can't carry 7 can swim 8 can walk
9 can't buy 10 can do

57b

1 Can you and Tom swim? we can't
2 Can Tom do karate? he can
3 Can your parents play tennis? they can't
4 Can your sister skate? she can't
5 Can you run fast? I can
6 Can you and Tom ski? we can

57c

Students' own answers

Unit 58

58a

1 Could Carla speak 2 couldn't read 3 could play
4 Could you see 5 couldn't say 6 could walk 7 could count
8 Could you use 9 couldn't swim 10 Could your sister write

58b

1 Could 2 could 3 can't 4 Can 5 can 6 couldn't 7 Can
8 can 9 couldn't 10 Could 11 could 12 can't

Unit 59

59a

1 Can I read your postcard?
2 Can we leave our bikes here?
3 Can I use your phone?
4 Can I open the window?
5 Can we sit at that table?
6 Can I keep this photo?
7 Can I tell her?
8 Can I look at your magazine?
9 Can we put our tent here?
10 Can we take the car?

59b

1 can 2 Can 3 can 4 Can 5 can't 6 Can 7 can 8 can
9 can't 10 can

Unit 60

60a

1 mustn't 2 must 3 mustn't 4 must 5 mustn't 6 mustn't

60b

1 mustn't bring 2 must write 3 must use 4 mustn't talk
5 must stay 6 mustn't copy 7 must stop 8 must give

Unit 61

61a

1 have to 2 has to 3 don't have to 4 don't have to 5 has to
6 doesn't have to 7 have to 8 doesn't have to 9 have to
10 don't have to

61b

1 Do we have to visit anybody?
2 Do you have to call Lisa?
3 Why does Ben have to have the car?
4 Do I have to help him and Sarah?
5 Do they have to leave early on Sunday?
6 Where does Sarah have to go?
7 Do we have to get any petrol?
8 Do you have to work on your project?

61c

1 have to 2 don't have to 3 have to 4 has to 5 doesn't have
to 6 Does he have to

61d

1 don't have to 2 mustn't 3 don't have to 4 mustn't
5 mustn't 6 don't have to 7 don't have to 8 mustn't

Check 11 Modal verbs (1)

1

1 Can 2 Could 3 can't 4 Can 5 couldn't

2

6 mustn't 7 have to 8 must 9 doesn't have to 10 mustn't

3

11 must 12 Can 13 can't 14 mustn't 15 don't have to

4

16 couldn't read 17 could learn 18 could play 19 can dance
20 can't practise

Unit 62

62a

1 Could you sign this card?
2 Could you move your chair?
3 Could you meet me at the station?
4 Could you turn off the TV?
5 Could you wait for me?
6 Could you hold this for a minute?
7 Could you give him my message?
8 Could you open the door?

62b

1 Can/Could you close   2 Can/Could you get   3 Can/Could you give   4 Can/Could you say   5 Can/Could you drive
6 Can/Could you ask

Unit 63

63a

1 I'll phone   2 I'll mend   3 I'll bring   4 I'll show   5 I'll buy
6 I'll make

63b

1 Shall I get you some aspirin?
2 Shall I go to the supermarket?
3 Shall I open the window?
4 Shall I come with you?
5 Shall I turn on the light?
6 Shall I ask him to phone you?

a 1   b 4   d 3   e 6   f 2   g 5

63c

1 Shall I bring   2 Shall I wash   3 I'll give   4 I'll show
5 Shall I carry   6 I'll make   7 I'll drive   8 Shall I turn on

Unit 64

64a

1 Let's buy   2 Shall we get   3 Let's walk   4 Let's wait   5 Shall we have   6 Shall we ask   7 Let's invite   8 Shall we listen

64b

1 How about   2 Why don't we   3 how about   4 Why don't we
5 how about   6 Why don't we

64c

1 Let's   2 What about   3 Shall we   4 Why don't we   5 Why don't we   6 Shall we   7 How about   8 Let's   9 How about
10 Let's

Unit 65

65a

1 shouldn't worry   2 should tell   3 should get up
4 shouldn't listen   5 shouldn't eat   6 should wear

65b

1 should I wear   2 should I buy   3 should I greet   4 Should I eat   5 should I sit   6 should I leave

65c

1 You should eat   2 You shouldn't drink   3 You should sleep
4 You shouldn't go   5 You shouldn't work   6 You should get

Unit 66

66a

1 We may not go to the beach.
2 Ryan may come here.
3 My parents may not be here.
4 We may watch a DVD.
5 James may join us.
6 We may not stay at home.
7 We may go to the cinema.
8 James may not come with us.

66b

1 may/might not have   2 may/might prefer   3 may/might not like   4 may/might know   5 may/might not stay   6 may/might stay

Check 12   Modal verbs 2

1

1 Shall   2 Should   3 I'll   4 Could   5 can

2

6 Let's sit   7 should drink   8 Can, take   9 might go
10 Shall, put

3

11 about   12 Shall   13 may/might   14 not   15 Can/Could

4

16 about listening   17 'll make   18 may/might not be
19 we look   20 may/might have

Unit 67

67a

Subject	Verb
A man	sang.
Kate	smiled.
We	left.

Subject	Verb	Object
We	loved	it.
She	liked	the songs.
I	bought	the CD.

Subject	Verb	Adverb
He	sang	beautifully.
Everybody	listened	carefully.
My brother	was	there.

Subject	Verb	Adjective
The tickets	*were*	*expensive.*
The music	was	fantastic.
We	were	amazed.

67b

1 She didn't want a sandwich.
2 Our exams start tomorrow.
3 Everybody worked hard.
4 They are having a party.
5 We spoke quietly.
6 Ryan was ill.
7 My cousins arrived yesterday.
8 He forgot his coat.

Unit 68

68a

1 She sent me <u>a postcard</u> from Paris.
2 She brought <u>Jo</u> some French chocolate.
3 She showed <u>us</u> her photos.
4 She gave me <u>a ring</u>.
5 And she bought Jo <u>a present</u> for her birthday.
6 She taught <u>us</u> some French words.

68b

1 I've brought you your book.
2 Sam offered me some cake.
3 They gave me some money.
4 I bought Sarah a CD.
5 We sent Becky a letter.
6 Adam lent me his jacket.
7 I'll show you my photos.
8 I got you a ticket.

68c

1 his chair to Matt   2 his guitar to me   3 his desk/table to Nikki   4 his bike/bicycle to Jamie   5 his TV/television to Rob   6 his bookcase/books to Lisa

68d

1 I've bought a CD for him.
2 We got Kelly some earrings.
3 I'm sending Tim a text message.
4 Lucy's made a cake for us.
5 We gave a big tip to the waitress.
6 Mark showed Alex his new bike.
7 They offered £1,000 to Jess.
8 Bring me that book.

Unit 69

69a

1 Use   2 do not feed   3 Call   4 Do not put   5 Do not walk   6 Take

69b

1 Don't go   2 take   3 don't forget   4 Say   5 Don't tell   6 Come

Unit 70

70a

1 there are   2 There isn't   3 There aren't   4 There's   5 There aren't   6 There isn't   7 There are   8 there's

70b

1 Is there   2 Are there   3 Are there   4 Is there   5 Is there   6 is there

70c

1 there aren't   2 There's   3 Is there   4 there is   5 There aren't   6 Are there   7 There are   8 there isn't

Unit 71

71a

1 It's   2 It isn't   3 is it   4 It's   5 is it   6 It isn't   7 is it   8 It isn't

71b

1 It was a long way   2 It's midnight   3 It's the 22nd 4 it was fine   5 it was wet   6 it was still dark   7 It's late   8 it's nice

71c

1 There's   2 It's   3 There's   4 is it   5 It's   6 There's   7 It's   8 There's

Check 13   Statements

1

1 We weren't talking loudly.
2 Jack hasn't got a bike.
3 She showed me her new phone.
4 The train was late.
5 Do not walk on the grass.

2

6 it   7 's   8 Do   9 There   10 it

3

11 There are   12 It's   13 there   14 There isn't   15 Don't

4

16 Have you bought <u>her</u> anything?
17 I got these earrings for <u>her</u> yesterday.
18 I love <u>them</u>!
19 I'm going to give <u>them</u> to her in the morning.
20 I'm going to give her <u>a CD</u>, I think.

Unit 72

72a

1 Do you need anything?
2 Could you open the window?
3 Have they gone with Adam?
4 Are you going to stay here?
5 Can I borrow this book?
6 Did he leave a message?
7 Will the campsite be full?
8 Have they got a dog?
9 Are you talking to me?
10 Was she waiting for you?

72b

1 Is Luke staying with Jack?
2 Can Jack take him to the match?
3 Have you met Luke?
4 Is he Kate's brother?
5 Does he live in Cambridge?
6 Were he and Jack at the same school?

72c
1 Do you do   2 Did you see   3 Did she phone   4 Do you know
5 Did she come   6 Does she work

72d
1 Do you like   2 Do you have   3 Have you got   4 Do you spend
5 Do they live   6 Do you make

Unit 73
73a
1 where   2 When   3 Why   4 How   5 why   6 How   7 Where
8 When

73b
1 Why   2 How   3 Where   4 How   5 When   6 Why   7 When
8 How   9 Why   10 Where

73c
1 How heavy   2 How often   3 How many   4 How wide
5 How big   6 How high

73d
1   How did you find it?
2   When did you get it?
3   How much did it cost?
4   Why did you choose this car?
5   How old is it?
6   How fast does it go?
7   How big is the engine?
8   How much petrol does it use?
9   Why do you need a car?
10 How often do you use it?

Unit 74
74a
1 What   2 Who   3 Which   4 Who   5 Whose   6 Which

74b
1 What colour   2 What size   3 What kind   4 What books
5 What day   6 What kind

74c
1 What   2 Which   3 What   4 Which   5 What   6 Which

74d
1 Who   2 What   3 Whose   4 Which   5 Whose   6 Who

74e
1   What sort of films do you like?   Students' own answer.
2   What kind of music do you like?   Students' own answer.
3   What is your favourite book?   Students' own answer.
4   Which sports can you play?   Students' own answer.
5   Who do you admire?   Students' own answer.
6   Whose advice do you follow?   Students' own answer.

Unit 75
75a
1   What's your course like?
2   What are your lecturers like?
3   What are the facilities like?
4   What's the sports centre like?
5   What was last term like?
6   What were your exams like?

75b
1   What was the weather like?
2   What was Marrakesh like?
3   What were the markets like?
4   What was your hotel like?
5   What was the food like?
6   What were the people like?

Check 14   Questions
1
1   Where have they gone?
2   What time is she coming?
3   Did he laugh?
4   Can I sit here?
5   How often do you go to town?

2
6 Did you go   7 What were the campsites   8 Were they
9 How much did they cost   10 Could I look

3
11 Which   12 How big   13 What   14 Where   15 What

4
16 What   17 How   18 Whose   19 Where   20 What

Unit 76
76a
1 Cycling   2 Running   3 sailing   4 Skating   5 Climbing
6 Camping

76b
1 Learning   2 Playing   3 Shopping   4 Doing   5 Talking
6 Following   7 Having   8 Being

Unit 77
77a
1 prefers cooking   2 don't mind tidying   3 love watching
4 likes getting up   5 doesn't like going   6 enjoy having

77b
1 visiting   2 having   3 reading   4 meeting   5 getting
6 working

Unit 78
78a
1 to be   2 to pass   3 to meet   4 to take   5 to organise
6 to bring   7 to go out   8 to drive

78b
1 to move   2 to live   3 to stay   4 to get   5 to speak
6 to improve

Unit 79
79a
1 would like to be   2 likes working   3 Would you like to go
4 would like to watch   5 like having   6 like listening
7 would you like to go   8 like living   9 Would you like to have
10 likes reading

79b

1 Would you like to come   2 'd like to visit   3 like staying   4 Do you like working   5 like helping   6 'd like to find

Unit 80

80a

1 i   2 c   3 g   4 a   5 h   6 e   7 d   8 f

80b

1 I'm going to Italy to improve my Italian.
2 I've stopped using my mobile phone to save money.
3 I've left the drama group to spend more time on my course.
4 I've joined a chat group to make some new friends.
5 I'm going to Germany to study Economics.
6 I'm writing to some colleges to ask about their courses.
7 I got a job as a waitress to earn some extra money.
8 I'm studying Psychology to understand the human mind.

Check 15 –ing forms and infinitives

1

1 to lose   2 Travelling   3 to look   4 to go   5 driving   6 working

2

7 to do   8 being   9 living   10 to make   11 eating   12 to try   13 walking   14 to visit

3

15 to buy   16 to read   17 to play   18 to cook   19 Watching   20 doing

4

21 to   22 like   23 Do   24 to   25 Would

Unit 81

81a

1 (that) our hotel rooms are   2 (that) the hotel's   3 (that) we can see   4 (that) there are   5 (that) the food's   6 (that) Emma brings   7 (that) Kim's got   8 (that) Emma's father can drive   9 (that) Emma's got   10 (that) Becky might come

81b

1 says, she loves   2 tells, her teachers are   3 says, the facilities are   4 tells, he doesn't like   5 says, it's   6 tells, he wants

81c

1 I'm sure (that) you'll be fine.
2 I'm certain (that) your performance will be brilliant.
3 I'm sorry (that) I won't see you.
4 I'm afraid (that) I have to go to London on Friday.
5 I'm afraid (that) I've promised to go to my uncle's 50th birthday party.
6 I'm certain (that) your concert will be a big success.
7 I'm sure (that) you've practised a lot.
8 I'm very sorry (that) I'll miss it.

Unit 82

82a

1 who   2 that   3 who   4 that   5 which   6 that   7 which   8 that   9 who   10 who

82b

1 The girl who/that sings in our band is very good.
2 The man who/that teaches me the guitar is a very good musician.
3 The friend who/that gave me her guitar bought a new one.
4 The people who/that came to our first gig enjoyed it.
5 The people who/that talked to us after the gig said nice things.

82c

1 Chalk is a kind of rock which/that is soft and white.
2 An eagle is a big, strong bird which/that eats meat.
3 A cactus is a plant which/that grows in hot dry places.
4 A giraffe is an animal which/that has a very long neck and long legs.
5 A glacier is a large quantity of ice which/that moves slowly down a valley.

82d

1 which/that divides the city in two   2 who/that took us to some interesting places   3 which/that crosses the river   4 who/that made lots of musical instruments   5 which/that lived in the ground   6 which/that are in the north

Unit 83

83a

1 The woman at the back is my grandmother.
2 The little boy in the middle is my brother.
3 The girl next to him is my cousin.
4 The man on the right is my dad.
5 The woman next to my dad is my aunt.

83b

1 with short dark hair is Becky   2 at the back is Lee   3 with glasses is Mark   4 at the front is Nicole   5 by/next to/near the lamp is Abby

Unit 84

84a

1 or   2 but   3 but   4 or   5 and   6 but   7 but   8 and   9 or   10 or

84b

1 so   2 because   3 because   4 because   5 so   6 so

84c

1 so   2 because   3 so   4 or   5 but   6 and

Unit 85

85a

1 After that   2 Next   3 Then   4 Next   5 after that   6 Finally

85b

a (3) Then/Next/After that   b (5) Then/Next/After that
c (0) First   d (6) Finally   e (1) Then/Next/After that
f (4) Then/Next/After that   g (2) Then/Next/After that

85c

1 Then/Next/After that, leave   2 then/next/after that, put
3 Then/Next/After that, measure   4 Then/Next/After that, buy
5 Then/Next/After that, move   6 Finally, paint

Unit 86

86a
1 'll sit 2 sit 3 won't eat 4 don't eat 5 'll phone 6 phone

86b
1 'll stay, don't feel 2 're, won't wait 3 go, 'll come
4 'll be, aren't 5 will you say, asks 6 won't see, leave

86c
1 If the train leaves London at twelve, it will be here at two.
2 If Lucy calls me, I'll ask her to come with us.
3 If you don't want to play tennis, we'll do something else.
4 If you need a tennis racket, I'll lend you mine.
5 If my brother isn't busy, he'll play with us.
6 If my dad finishes work early, he'll drive us to the sports centre.
7 If it rains, we'll stay at home.
8 If you're interested, I'll show you my paintings.
9 If you like my paintings, I'll draw a picture of you.
10 If Matt lets us use his computer, we'll visit Jo's new website.

86d
1 'll find 2 make 3 won't forget 4 don't take 5 'll feel
6 won't work 7 divide 8 'll do 9 plan 10 won't worry

Unit 87

87a
1 leave 2 Will you call 3 'll be 4 see 5 starts 6 'll be 7 sign
8 'll talk

87b
1 I'll make, they arrive 2 I buy, I'll ask 3 will he do, he leaves
4 Will you have, you start 5 I'll decide, I know 6 I'll have, I go
7 I go, I'll get 8 He'll call, he gets 9 We'll visit, we leave
10 I'll call, I get

Check 16 Clauses

1
1 get 2 meet 3 'll see 4 won't do 5 hear 6 'll play 7 'll be

2
8 and 9 who 10 which 11 so 12 after that 13 that 14 says
15 Finally

3
16 Then/Next 17 in 18 that 19 or 20 on 21 that 22 'll
23 who/that 24 but 25 which/that

Unit 88

88a
1 on 2 at 3 on 4 in 5 in 6 at 7 in 8 on

88b
1 in the bowl 2 on the wall 3 at the table 4 on the chair
5 in the/her bag 6 at the window 7 in the kitchen 8 on the table

88c
1 at 2 in 3 in 4 in 5 on 6 on

Unit 89

89a
1 above 2 next to 3 under 4 in front of 5 near 6 behind

89b
1 next to 2 among 3 above 4 opposite 5 between
6 behind 7 next to 8 near

89c
1 in front of 2 opposite 3 near 4 between 5 behind
6 above 7 under 8 among

Unit 90

90a
1 up 2 onto 3 across 4 into 5 down 6 to

90b
1 from the beach 2 down the hill 3 onto the boat 4 out of the cinema 5 across the bridge

90c
1 down 2 out of 3 to 4 off 5 onto 6 from

90d
1 to 2 across 3 down 4 off 5 into 6 out of

Unit 91

91a

on	in	at
14th April	1999	Easter
my birthday	August	half past three
Saturday	the evening	noon
Thursday morning	the summer	the moment

91b
1 at 2 in 3 In 4 in 5 At 6 on

91c
1 in 2 – 3 at 4 – 5 – 6 on

91d
1 at, on, ✗ 2 on, ✗ 3 on, ✗ 4 at, in, ✓ 5 On, at, ✓

91e
Students' own answers

Unit 92

92a
1 after 2 during 3 before 4 After 5 before 6 during
7 after 8 during

92b
1 for 2 during 3 for 4 during 5 for 6 for 7 during
8 during

Check 17 Prepositions of place, movement and time

1
1 on 2 onto 3 in 4 out of 5 during

2
6 on 7 next to 8 behind 9 between 10 in front of

3
11 on   12 at   13 off   14 in   15 before
4
16 at   17 in   18 After   19 to   20 –

Unit 93
93a
1 in   2 on   3 in   4 by   5 at   6 on   7 by   8 in   9 on   10 by
93b
1 in   2 on   3 at   4 in   5 by   6 by   7 at   8 at   9 in   10 on
93c
1 in France   2 by air   3 by boat   4 at university   5 at school
6 in bed

Unit 94
94a
1 e   2 f   3 d   4 g   5 a   6 b
94b
1 of   2 by   3 of   4 with   5 about   6 in   7 at   8 about   9 to
10 to
94c
1 at   2 about   3 to   4 with   5 with   6 of

Unit 95
95a
1 off   2 for   3 at   4 in   5 on   6 down   7 back   8 off
95b
1 set off   2 went on   3 broke down   4 gave up   5 rang up
6 came round

Check 18   Prepositions and phrasal verbs
1
1 on   2 out   3 in   4 with   5 out   6 of
2
7 for   8 at   9 with   10 up   11 on   12 of
3
13 on   14 in   15 off   16 on   17 at   18 in   19 down   20 by

Unit 96
96a
1 tired   2 amazing   3 bored   4 surprised   5 relaxing   6 excited
96b
1 boring   2 interested   3 relaxed   4 frightening   5 exciting
6 amazing

Unit 97
97a

-y		-able		-ful	
health	*healthy*	fashion	fashionable	success	successful
cloud	cloudy	count	countable	pain	painful
noise	noisy	enjoy	enjoyable	colour	colourful
fun	funny	wash	washable	help	helpful
salt	salty	accept	acceptable	wonder	wonderful
dust	dusty	value	valuable	hope	hopeful

97b
1 enjoyable   2 sunny   3 beautiful   4 comfortable   5 useful
6 careful   7 stony   8 sleepy

Unit 98
98a
1 unkind   2 impossible   3 unnecessary   4 impolite
5 imperfect   6 unusual
98b
1 unfriendly   2 impatient   3 unfashionable   4 unpopular
5 impossible   6 unsuccessful
98c
Students' own answers

Unit 99
99a
1 bus stop   2 clothes shop   3 tennis ball   4 mountain bike
5 car park   6 computer game
99b
1 sunglasses   2 hairbrush   3 notebook   4 motorbike
5 newspaper   6 noticeboard   7 backpack   8 tracksuit

Check 19   Word formation
1
1 useful   2 impatient   3 enjoyable   4 dirty   5 unkind
2
6 frightened   7 surprised   8 amazing   9 relaxed   10 bored
3
11 Internet café   12 Art project   13 sports centre   14 bus stop
15 music shop
4
16 comfortable   17 beautiful   18 unusual   19 cloudy
20 impossible